AS A KITE FALLS
A Voyage Through Descent

Richard Tyler

Finding hope in the darkest of times

KARNAC
firing the mind

First published in 2024 by
Karnac Books Limited
62 Bucknell Road
Bicester
Oxfordshire OX26 2DS

British Library Cataloguing in Publication Data

A C.I.P. for this book is available from the British Library

ISBN: 978-1-80013-268-9 (paperback)
ISBN: 978-1-80013-269-6 (e-book)
ISBN: 978-1-80013-270-2 (PDF)

Typeset by vPrompt eServices Pvt Ltd, India

Printed in the United Kingdom

www.firingthemind.com

Praise for *As A Kite Falls*

In a world that is awash with success messaging, it is refreshing and inspirational to read such a beautifully written account on how to overcome and find acceptance in the dips and pitfalls of this life. Richard is spreading a vital, motivational, and hopeful message which will nestle into your soul vision and work its way into your heart, if you let it.

Donna Ashworth, author of *The Sunday Times*
No. 1 bestseller *Wild Hope*

Richard Tyler gives us a fearless account of what it is like to truly be human! A soul journey of the heart that transports you into his ever fluent world. His engaging humour and true transparency is gut wrenching, heartbreaking, and courageous. No stone is left unturned but nor could it be when one has walked a path such as his. His creative honesty allows us to truly see inside of ourselves at the same time. To not be alone, an outsider, or a bystander. We walk, cry, laugh, and dance with him. Yet as he plays the game of life, we are left on the edge of our seats wondering outcomes. What will happen next? Where will he take us? A real story, a true story and yet everyone's story in some way or another. He brings humanity together with one voice.

Nadine Benjamin, professional opera singer, leadership and empowerment coach/mentor, and speaker

As the old liturgy has it, in the midst of life we are in death. We all wish for ascent without its necessary companion descent. Richard Tyler shares his experience of both. One cannot come away from reading his account without a deeper consideration of life's paradox: that there is no ascent without descent as well. What matters is not the venue for our appointments with descent; what matters is how we go through the fire, how we come to accept the unacceptable, and how the depth, dignity, and degradation of this journey is accompanied by grace, hope, and occasionally even love.

James Hollis, PhD, Jungian analyst,
Washington, DC, and author

Richard beautifully encapsulates both the drama and mundanity of living with a cancer and its treatment. His book takes us through a sometimes brutal depiction of illness and treatment and how that felt like a 'descent' following what he describes as a life of achievement and privilege.

The themes throughout the book are also ones we see every day in our centres from people with cancer—the realisation that you can slow life down and leave space for small things that bring joy, like appreciating nature and the seasons. And the importance of finding hope, not just for yourself but for family, partners, and children.

While the book is about Richard's descent from his former success to his new life as a person with cancer, I found it to be a hopeful read about how cancer, despite all its darkness, can bring with it new beginnings, a fresh perspective, and stronger relationships with those you love and who love you back.

Dame Laura Lee, Chief Executive, Maggie's

There is no doubt that I've lived through my own fair share of descent. As an Olympic boxing medalist, I knew what it was like to be pushed to achieve more, punch harder, and be stronger. But with all of that comes the fall—the moments where our world crashes. Through his words, Richard has captured the essence of not only his own story, but the universal one that most of us were taught as we grew up: go faster, go harder, go bigger. He provides us with an important lesson—we must support our future generations to not only climb higher, but to also find ways to be with our own crashing descent. Descent is an opportunity to learn, build awareness, and to adapt. It's not what happens to you, it's how you choose to face it.

Anthony Ogogo, Olympic boxing medallist

Richard Tyler peels away the layers of his life to reveal the rawness and vulnerability that we all face as humans. As a triple amputee and having been pronounced dead not once, but twice, I have seen the effects of my own world coming to a crashing halt. But with enormous will, support, and a deep belief that we are limitless, I continue to thrive and win at life. Richard so elegantly reminds us through his use of haiku, that when we are stripped back to our nakedness, an extraordinary quality of resolve and determination is unleashed. This is not available to just a gifted few, it is available to us all.

Mark Ormrod, MBE, Invictus Games athlete, author, and motivational speaker

Richard writes in such a way that you feel as though you are a friend going on his journey with him. Not sure what to say or do to help, but you're alongside him. He writes candidly and there will be something in Richard's writing that will resonate with everyone. It is one heck of a journey but you will be grateful to read it and grateful Richard has shared it.

Gail Porter, TV personality

Foreword
Brett Kahr

Nowadays, very few of us will be capable of reading a full-length book in just one sitting, but, within minutes of having embarked upon Richard Tyler's deeply moving, extremely well-written and unusually honest memoir, *As a Kite Falls: A Voyage Through Descent*, I simply could not stop doing so, and I absorbed this important new publication with warm emotion and deep appreciation.

As a young, lithe, popular star of the West End stage, who appeared in such iconic musicals as *Les Misérables* and *The Phantom of the Opera*, Richard Tyler led an absolutely perfect life throughout much of his twenties and thirties, adored by many female admirers, and blessed with a beautiful young daughter to boot. However, in 2021, he received a shocking and horrifying medical diagnosis which threatened his life.

I have worked for nearly half a century in the mental health field, and during this time I have had the privilege of supporting and treating numerous patients who suffered from cancers, brain tumours and other dreaded conditions. Many of these individuals had, alas, broken down completely in the wake of their illnesses, and some even developed schizophrenia or other forms of psychosis in addition to their medical diseases.

Fortunately, Richard had grown up in a loving family and had enjoyed a lifetime of creativity and accomplishment, which provided him with a sufficiently sturdy ego structure. Moreover, after he had achieved many years of success working in musical theatre, Tyler embarked upon an engaging career as a businessman and as an author, and even pursued psychotherapy in his own right; hence, he had already spent much transformative time in what I have come to refer to as the 'psychological gym', developing his mental muscles in many unique ways. Thankfully, that emotional bedrock permitted him to survive his lymphoma diagnosis in the most brave and bold manner possible.

As Richard explains, the shock of his illness proved utterly devastating, but he has, thankfully, soldiered through, due to the love of those near and dear to him, due to the care that he received from his doctors and nurses, and, perhaps most of all, as a result of his inner strength and his capacity to use the illness as an opportunity to engage in creative projects, rather than to succumb to despair and hopelessness.

With immense honesty and generosity, Richard Tyler has graciously chosen to share these private insights with us all. Rather memorably, he has focused with much lucidity on the challenges that confront every single one of us as human beings, namely, the inevitable struggle between *descent* and *ascent* across our lifetimes. Such insights will resonate with every single mortal human being. And those of us who work as psychologists, psychotherapists, psychiatrists, psychoanalysts, social workers, counsellors, nurses, occupational therapists or physicians will, I hope, become even more empathic, as—thanks to this book— we develop an even greater understanding of the nature of life-threatening illness and the potential for survival.

Having spent many decades in academia, immersing myself in zillions of classic texts, I can think of few tomes as compelling as this one. I hope that we shall all treat ourselves to Richard's warmth and wisdom and that we will join him on this transformative journey, which affects all eight billion of us.

Professor Brett Kahr
Senior Fellow, Tavistock Institute of Medical Psychology, London
Honorary Director of Research, Freud Museum London

To all those
who happen to find themselves
somewhere on the journey
between no longer and not yet ...

Note to the reader

Many are drawn to reading this book as they are experiencing tough times, those that include grief, loss, hardship, illness or disappointment.When you feel like your life is crumbling apart, it can be hard to stand face to face with the treacherous path ahead. But whilst most of us are taught the art of *ascent*, we are rarely taught the lessons in how to handle times of *descent*.

I trust that my story will act as your beacon of hope. Just like the Japanese word *kintsugi* encourages you to embrace the old and the battered, and to join the broken pieces together with gold and make something even more beautiful, this book is an attempt to reassemble the shattered mosaic of my own life, into something even more beautiful.

My intention is to help you lean into the emotions that you've previously been told to block out, encouraging you to approach them with curiosity, humour and creativity, as there is gold and healing in this often unexplored terrain.

In the darkest of times, keep the faith. The sun always rises. Open your mind, your heart and be a vessel for love.

I think our journey together has already begun …

One

'**O**k, go!' I shout out to dad that I'm ready. He takes a few of his funny running steps and, whoosh, he sends the kite up up up. If I am quick, I will catch a glimpse of his smile, his own childlike wonder, sprint across from one cheek to the other.

For a few beautiful moments, I indulge in the effortless pursuit of flight. My kite, that I'm piloting, twists and turns and somersaults. Like a swallow in motion, twirling and rolling at speed. Inside, I secretly whoop. Not to the outside world of course. There is no place for such brazen displays of joy. But in my heart I wish for this fleeting moment to last a lifetime. I am elated. Dad is elated. And for these few precious seconds at least, nothing else matters …

The moment is short lived. Soon after the up up up, I am eaten alive by the down down down. Maybe my kite is overwhelmed by its own fear of heights as it appears hell-bent on getting back down to earth via the shortest possible route. With all my might, I valiantly fight to keep it airborne. The seconds slow to a near standstill. I skip. I run. I freeze. I drop my hands. I lift them high. But no, the kite doesn't care. It has just one destination.

Almost taking my dad out, it crashes hard into the grass. And that's when I see it. In this moment, everything changes. I watch as his joy morphs into something else. 'Christ alive!'

I am never entirely sure if he is actually blaming Christ or just calling for his assistance. A few seconds of waiting for Christ to appear and, nope, nothing happens. He collects the kite, marches back to me, preparing for a debrief. My best day suddenly edges closer towards being my worst. My own joy, like the kite, is brought to a crashing halt.

If I'm lucky, we'll head straight home. If I'm unlucky, we'll repeat this whole exercise. A quiet drive back follows. In my heart, I hold the beauty that Coombe Hill has shown me. Alongside it sits the heaviness of not quite understanding who my dad is most disappointed with: the kite, the weather, his own kite skills, the days he missed out on without his own father present, or me.

———————◆———————

If you've never been to Coombe Hill, hidden away in the Chilterns, it's worth a visit. On a clear day, the views steal your breath. I would almost explode with excitement as I skipped up the path to the monument at the top of the hill. Kite held aloft, I secretly bubbled with joy. I was out with my dad and here we were, blessed with the perfect conditions for kites to soar. What could possibly go wrong?! My little heart could hardly consume the magnificence and beauty of the wispy blue sky and the almost fluorescent summer green grass. And here I was, right in it and ready to play. Kite in one hand, dad's hand in the other.

To this small 7-year-old, it felt like I was on top of the world. Literally. Dad didn't like flying so we'd never travelled in a plane. Being on the top of Coombe Hill was like soaring sky high. If I stretched up just enough, I was sure I could tickle the armpit of the clouds. I would tentatively move towards the edge of the hill, terrified that I might drop off the other side. And at the same time, desperately hoping that we could find the best gust of wind that would carry my small orange kite high up into the clouds.

I'd follow my dad's guidance to the letter. He seemed to know more about flying kites than I did. In most instances, we agreed that he was better at the launching of the kite and I was more suited to the steering. I'm unsure how we concluded that to be that case. But it's how it was.

The words 'Christ alive!' are deeply etched into my gut. He'd regularly express his pent-up frustration this way: washing up, me knocking the heads off his roses with a football, my mum's poor timekeeping and our kite-flying. Or should I say, our kite-falling? I could always read his frustration, even when I couldn't quite hear his mutterings. His stature altered. He stooped. He stiffened. I felt it as anger. Or was it annoyance? Perhaps disgust. Disappointment? I'm not sure. After all, what is any 7-year-old sure of?

I've often wondered what childhood was like for my dad. He lost his own father when he was 7, to then be packed off to a boarding school with his younger brother in tow. His mother never oozed a tender, kind and loving energy. She had to cope with losing her husband and was left with two young boys to raise, alone. Where did her own love come from? And who taught my dad to fly his kite? Who was present enough to help him navigate the ups and downs of his life? I imagine he was left to figure out much of it for himself. With a boarding school environment of the 1940s, World War II as the backdrop, maybe it wasn't a hot house for growing love and compassion. My dad was a man fixated on success. He strived for the ups. He was the eternal seeker of ascent. His own sense of worth was entwined with how well he was doing. When I stand back and look at the rich patchwork of his upbringing, I can see how a crashing kite could be difficult to bear.

Two

It seems as if we've all become fixated on the up up up; living in hot pursuit of ascent. Climb aloft. Get more. Say *Yes!* to everything. Fly higher. Faster. Bigger. Better. More light. More beauty. More love. More more more. Our culture does, after all, honour the winners.

It's all high fives, cheerleaders and whooping. Cupcakes and Bollinger. Wide smiles. Man hugs with back-slapping. Celebration. Joy. A lightness pervades as we ascend. Climbing to the dizzy heights of victory. We have become obsessed with raising everything up.

This was certainly the familiar and heady waters I swam in during my early career as an actor.

I never settled with the roles I was given, I wanted a better one. *The* better one. I chased the next. And the next. There was little satisfaction with *this one*. I just wanted *that one*.

Being a successful actor means working once or twice in your lifetime. It's a precarious business where the lucky few get to work *on* the stage as opposed to *in* the auditorium selling ice creams. I was one of those lucky few. Bloody lucky in fact. I had a great agent, looked half decent and had the most superb hair. I always said that it was my hair that got me the gigs! I had winner written all over me.

I played in many theatrical phenomenons. I got standing ovations. I signed programmes. I signed T-shirts. Heck, I even signed a total stranger's pants that she sent me in a discreet jiffy envelope. And each time I was offered a new gig, I'd do a secret fist pump, stand a little taller, stare into the mirror and tell myself how wonderful I was. Beyond that moment, I'd say nothing more about it. *No one likes a smarty pants.*

I played some of the biggest roles in musical theatre: *Les Misérables*, *Phantom of the Opera*. I sang in a handful of the best venues across the globe: Sydney Opera House, The Royal Albert Hall. I can safely say that in my time, I lived a few ups!

In the spring of 2000, as the world reeled from fireworks and feasting to bring in the new millennium, I was busy living through my own meltdown. It was a kind of midlife crisis. Except I was 29. I masked it well and dressed it up for others under the guise of wanting to find something new in my life. In reality, I was lost. Tired. Battle weary from auditions and the relentless treadmill of 8 shows a week. In what felt like a hasty move, I burnt bridges, left my agent, dramatically swished my scarf around my neck and flounced off stage right.

My mum was mortified. Oh, not for me and my emotional turmoil. No, she just had no idea what on earth to tell her hairdresser. A massive void opened up in her life where she had at one time regaled her friends with stories of her super successful son. Now he was lost. And not a success. In fact, he was unemployed. And had no vocation. Who wants to brag to their friends about that?

At this time, my urge for yet more *up* found me sliding down. In the pit of my gut, I believed there was something else to discover, a different way to utilise my talents. What were my talents? Tap dancing, telling stories and making music. The options appeared somewhat limited.

Through a chance meeting and my own bravery to say *fuck it* when some weird opportunity was revealed to me, I pivoted into organisational training and development. I have spent the last 23 years studying the psyche. I trained in Barrett Values, various psychometric tools, cognitive hypnotherapy, CBT, NLP and emotional intelligence. Laterally, I trained as a psychotherapist at the Psychosynthesis Trust, London. All in an effort to dig deeper into the human condition, to help connect myself and others with their innate but often illusive sense of purpose and calling.

Throughout this second chapter of my career, I've used my knowledge and experience to deliver training and keynotes to some of the biggest corporate brands on the planet. I published *Jolt*, a book to help move people out of their comfort zones into a place where they can be something more, something different, their unique selves. My team and I travelled to every continent to help leaders and their organisations rediscover their balance and alignment.

In all of this journeying however, the focus remained on attaining and helping others seek and access positivity, optimism and a better life. More ascent. More ups.

As is the case for all of us, scattered throughout this play we each star in, entitled *My Life*, I have not been without my share of scenes that are heavy with descent. What I have come to realise is that both personally and as a society, we lack the framework and language to be able to fully inhabit the emotional spectra our lives traverse. Consequently, we are neither able to enjoy and learn from our ups or sit with our downs long enough to listen to the beauty they too have to offer. In Greek mythology, this journeying down into the underworld is called *katabasis*.

These journeys are deemed to be a vital component of life and without them, there can be no *anabasis*—the adventure back up.

Imagine a tall house. One that boasts both a roof terrace and a cellar. Hiding away in the dark chilly basement, in the deepest bowels of the house, lies our shadow. It is here where we store our primitive urges and fundamental drivers. It is a place of deep emotion. Think of it as the birthplace for manifestations such as phobias, compulsive urges and delusions. All that we have lived through that feels too heavy to bear is placed here. We box it up and push it down. We repress it. And as we flee our own shadow, so we flee ourselves. The basement soon becomes the uncomfortable part of the house that we don't talk about and certainly don't venture down into.

At the very top of the house, you will find the roof terrace. A place of light, intuition and inspiration. The space where our greater human potential awaits our attention. Qualities such as love, forgiveness and acceptance reside here—they wait patiently to be unlocked and set free. Whilst we assume the bottom of the house is the hardest place to occupy, the same can be true with the top of the house.

In an effort to dampen down the joy, the light and to extinguish the flame of our own potential, we stop visiting the roof terrace quite so often too. The basement overflows and our shadow starts to seep up and onto the ground floor. Much like bind weed, everything in sight becomes entangled in its clutches. Ascending the stairs to the roof, even with sun protection and shades, is painfully bright. The light drenches the top floors and in our discomfort and vulnerability, we turn away.

We stop venturing up. We stop venturing down. It is not long until our life centres only around the middle floor. Here, our awareness is easily accessible. Memories are easy to retrieve and what enters our imagination can start to take some form if, of course, we allow it. And so we end up occupying a tiny slither of our existence. We function. Just. We normalise it. We smile and show the outside world just how happy we are living in our 3-storey house, masking the reality that our life is being lived predominantly on just one floor. It is a provisional existence.

This is the house that most of us end up living in.

Avoiding the lows, the dark, the shadow parts of ourselves might on one level seem to make sense. The discomfort we feel in this area is obvious and often visceral. As a therapist, it is all too clear to me, however, that we can so easily end up burying the highs too. We fear our own greatness. Neither the light nor the dark are our enemy. Our resistance to them, though, is.

French psychotherapist Robert Desoille coined the phrase, *the repression of the sublime*. We are tricked into thinking that repression only applies to the darker materials of our tapestry: loss, guilt, isolation, shame. We disown that part of ourselves because including it is unbearable. We split it off from the rest of who we are.

My experience tells me that we can just as easily disown our beauty and our gifts, as much as we can our ugliness and our limitation. Pure joy and ecstasy can feel too much to hold; all eyes upon us as we writhe around, screeching in orgasmic delight. Does society have a tendency to shun the essence of other people's ascent and judge it as arrogant or showing off? After all, no one likes those suffering with Tall Poppy Syndrome. And, because venturing down the stairs into our own basement is too scary, we derive pleasure from gawping at other people's lows instead.

Perhaps seeing how successful *you* are means that I look towards my own success and then measure the two. I did that.

I'd look at other actors, see that they got the gig, watch them smile and gloat, and then despise them for it. 'Break a leg,' I'd say, cheerily, through clenched teeth. Secretly hoping that they would, in fact, break their leg. I cannot believe I have just admitted that to you.

Global sales of self-help books tops $11 billion annually. Online learning is pumped full of over $250 billion of our cash. That, along with a cult-like hunger for personal development gurus, some of whom are worth over $500 billion, there is clearly an appetite for improvement. For a better life. For more joy. More sex. More homes. More money. More happiness. More soaring kites. For ascent. We are literally buying the blueprint for success.

I don't see the same voracious appetite for shadow exploration, yet the shadow continues to pulsate. The basement door bulges. Buy as many self-help books as you like and dream of sitting out on the roof, Pina Colada in hand, celebrating reaching the top. I did this. I did exactly this for years. I could hear the basement door creak and yet no amount of liberal smearing of Vaseline or vigorous spraying of WD-40, would soothe it. And eventually, it exploded. The door was blown off. But I'll come to that part in good time.

I wonder what it might it be like if we celebrated both ascent *and* descent? What if, rather than repressing and burying the difficulties that come with the fall, we include them in our life as a source of insight and information? Something that requires the same delicate handling as the highs.

Joseph Campbell taught us well in *The Hero's Journey* about how we are presented with many adventures and missions throughout our lifetime. Here we get to see first-hand how, if we choose to accept the mission, life will present us with a series of opportunities. The reality is that some will go up. Some will go down. I don't recall the point where he taught us that this is binary; one is good and one is bad. It seems, though, that society has taken on that narrative. Up reflects success, confidence and ease. Down is our story of hardship, pain and suffering.

The key to repossessing the whole house, our whole selves, lies in the basement. This book is about sharing what emerged for me when I was finally faced with a descent that I could not close the door on. From it, I offer the promising possibility that there's something on offer for each of us, some gifts we can't elucidate or know until we give ourselves over entirely to our descent. Until we summon the courage to sit in the dark with ourselves. To be the hero in our own journey.

Descent leads us down into an unfamiliar geography. It is a mapless terrain. In the old language of Alchemy, we cross into the Nigredo, the Blackening. The place where the shadow lives. This is very much a season of decay, of shedding and endings, of falling apart and undoing.

I've buried my own falling down many times in life. The shame, despair and embarrassment I felt was often unbearable. On the flip side, despite chasing the highs, I would never allow myself to roll around in them for fear of being called a show-off. So I opted to bury the highs too. This left me living in some kind of no man's land; stowing away the downs and hiding any trace of the ups. It was this. Or that. It was life on the first floor.

I had no language and no model that guided me towards including *both/and,* as opposed to simply *either/or.* I was trying to function within a binary system that either praised me or scolded me. There is none more prolific than our education system: pass/fail, right/wrong, good/bad. I *failed* my 11+. I watched as my friends whooped and cheered. I watched their families shower them with gifts and praise. One of my friends

12

got a Tamiya Hotshot II Blockhead remote-controlled car. I refused to play with it and, for a few days, with him. Me? I just sobbed. I sobbed my heart out. I saw the disappointment fill my parents' eyes as I broke the news. They didn't know what to say. I don't even recall what words they used. I just remember the moment right before it; the fleeting sigh, the exasperation, their inability to voice how they felt. Maybe this was my first conscious brush with being seen as a disappointment. Anyway, in true British style, we quickly moved on and it was never spoken about again.

At the end of Act I of my life, aged a little over 40, came a crushing divorce and split from my daughter's mother. After many years of struggle and tussle in an attempt to realign, the curtain finally fell on our marriage. It was, for me, a massive relief. Painful, and still a relief. No one likes to fall in the face of defeat. But it was a fall that I believed I could soothe. My lungs re-filled to capacity and I could, once more, catch my breath. My body felt lighter than it had done for years. It was a relationship that had become massively out of balance. My own values had become compromised and I'd woken one day finding myself living a life of constriction.

I was scared to choose. Scared to make a decision. Scared to ask for what I wanted. I lived in service of my young daughter and yet I compromised her happiness in order to make decisions that would appease my then wife. I had lost of sight of who I was. I had ventured so far away from my true nature, I was off course and lost in barren land. The silent psychological and emotional toll this took was catastrophic. It's akin to trauma. Actually, it IS trauma.

Years later, here I am still working through the remnants and remains of something that resembled a war zone with a few vases of flowers and some incense sticks; each strategically

13

placed to make the overall look feel more like something from *Elle Decoration*. Yet, if you peered a little closer, you could see the death and decay. I felt ashamed by a failing relationship so chose to hide it deep in the basement of my life. Each day I would venture down to store a bit more of my noisy existence that had become unbearable. There was little joy to be seen. For anyone.

I went into therapy. I was mortified that I couldn't solve this puzzle by myself. Each week, for 60 precious minutes I would sit with Amita and she would help me to unravel and unknot some of the bindweed. For the first time in years, I felt like I stood in a place of presence. I started to occupy the here and now. I peered down into the basement of my life and looked up to the sky to imagine the potential. Through it all, Amita stood firm. She held me to account when I reneged on my commitments and she showed me love when the hurt was too intense.

I had always chased ascent. I sought out the eternal highs that supposedly come with better, more and moving on up: success, recognition, adoration, creativity, jobs and love. Yes, probably love. How could I find a relationship where I could give more love and receive more love. The hot pursuit of a smouldering relationship took me down many deep ravines and up some small mounds!

It took me 42 years to find Kelly. My beloved. My soulmate. My best friend. I knew she was somewhere in the crowd, but as hard as I tried, I had not been able to locate her. In the intervals between Acts I and II of my life, we found each other. She's here now and we very firmly walk alongside each other on our respective solo and joint paths. But only when I stopped pursuing the eternal road of love and ascent did she become visible.

What I am discovering, very slowly, is that until we open the door to our basement and incorporate the shadow into our life, truthful ascent and joy remain out of reach. The shadow work is vital. Including it means we get to ascend the steps towards the roof terrace. It is on our roof terrace where the beauty and the light wait to be stirred by us. Here, like Sleeping Beauty, our potential joy of life is waiting for us to kiss it back into existence.

Being human hurts. Whilst ascent and descent are neither good nor bad, we would much rather follow the thread of positivity that ascent seduces us with. But by doing this, do we end up inviting one in and banishing the other? The reality is that being positive does not solve every human problem. When I look back through my own childhood, I see 2 parents who struggled with their own responses to the ups and downs that life threw at them. I often wonder how they would have lived their own lives differently if they'd learned an alternative narrative around falling up *and* falling down. The myths we have created around these leave many of us entangled amongst the toxic stories of our familial systems.

Sooner or later in life, we will all descend. Broken relationships, redundancy, loss, rejection, illness and ultimately, death. Sadly though, it seems we only teach people how to ascend and rise in their life. We fail to show ways to better manage the descent. We don't educate people to open their basement door before it bursts. Whilst this calls upon us to cultivate great courage and will in order to grasp the handle, there is no denying that descent is a precarious path to walk. Perhaps we can take heart from the words of Ovid, the Roman poet, who reminded us to *be patient and tough; some day this pain will be useful to you.*

This book takes you on a journey *through* descent. My journey. My descent. Not *around* descent. And not *of* descent. But purposefully *through* it. It is crammed with intimate moments that I want to share with you because I want to show you what happens when you value, make space and celebrate both the ups and the downs. Descent is the portal through which we find the meaning within our life. Our shadow can be converted into light if we are open to staying with it until it transforms. We don't have to just float above ourselves, being the voyeur to the action on stage.

So, strap yourself in. You are invited to find your own courage and turn towards your soul. Some people experience the word *soul* as having religious undertones. I watch them flinch. I simply refer to it as meaning my true essence: my deepest nature, quintessence, Self, spirit—who I am most at my core. You will find me using the word a fair bit during the book but it is interchangeable with whatever word works for you.

My hope is that *As a Kite Falls* will stir something within you enough to inspect the mosaic of your own existence. Some of what I say may be pure food for thought. It might massage your thinking and pierce your heart. The rest of it will perhaps offer some medicine for your soul. And at no time more than this do we need to be reunited with that deepest aspect of ourselves.

Real life doesn't have to be just big, bright and splashy. My hope is that in whatever way we each choose to walk our path, we can perhaps do so by valuing and understanding that as our kite may fly, so our kite must fall. And pure beauty exists in both.

Three

Decemeber 7th, 2021 is the tattoo on my body that I never asked for. It was the day my world crashed around me. Each tiny turn saw another fragile aspect of my life rupture.

We knew there were some mysterious goings-on in my body in the June of 2021. A gut flare-up, a UTI or two, some weight loss, the odd drenching night sweat. Mostly, I felt well. Life continued. Kelly and I celebrated our 4th wedding anniversary in Cornwall. I worked. Mia, our daughter, had her summer holidays, preparing to start her A-levels in the September. I quite liked the new, streamlined waist I was sporting. It gave me that upside-down V-shape that the gym trainer had promised me back in 1994; superhero-esque. Just 25 years later than I'd expected. And, seemingly, this time without any effort. Result.

When the multiple cycles of antibiotics no longer worked their magic, I asked to see a urologist. A scan, some bloods and an ultrasound revealed an enlarged, left-sided inguinal lymph node (buried deep in my groin). The radiologist compared the scan with one from a few years ago when I had kidney stones (one of the many taps on the shoulder that my soul had given me—and yes, I didn't pay attention). The node was now outside of safe limits. I was hastily referred to a haematologist.

More bloodletting activities, a CT and a PET scan that lit up like Oxford Street at Christmas followed. Whilst this went on, I started to experience a deep pain in my left hip and down the side of my leg. As the days crept by, I began to feel more and more rough. The haematologist requested a biopsy of the lymph. It was not going to be easy surgery as it was so deeply hidden away. Every day brought new challenges: additional pain, more night sweats, the torturous wait for biopsy results, a family Covid adventure, a 5-day retreat in Kingston Hospital to manage my pain and a stash of morphine from my GP. My gentle and kind haematologist continued to reassure us that it was probably nothing; 'maybe a lazy lymphoma,' he chimed.

At 3 pm on December 6th, out of sheer desperation, Kelly chased the biopsy results. Our haematologist explained that the results were only just back and he'd now like me to see a different haematologist, one that specialised in oncology. She'd call us. At 5 pm, she did just that. 'I'll see you at 9 am tomorrow please. And do you have any steroids in the house that you could start on now?!' I mean, who has a box of steroids lying around, just waiting to spring into action? Anyway, there are not many things more fear-inducing than an oncology consultant requesting your immediate presence.

'You have cancer'; 3 short words that can wreak havoc across an entire landscape. And 3 short words that I thought would never be uttered to me. Whilst I remain baffled that my dad got cancer in 2011, I have made up all kinds of stories as to why that might have been so and a handful of stories to enforce why I would not get cancer. It seems that the beautiful tales we can tell ourselves do not always present as the truth …

As expected, a lymphoma diagnosis followed. What was unexpected was the ugliness of it all. Stage 4b, Mantle Cell Lymphoma; a rare and aggressive cancer that affects only a few hundred people in the UK each year. I would have to be fussy and be given something *rare*. In this moment, I'd have opted for something boring and mainstream. But there was no choice. Treatment would begin the next day. 'If you don't have treatment, you'll have a few months left.' I stopped listening from here. A further 3 hours of form filling, blood-taking, drug giving and general fiddling went mainly unnoticed by me. I deferred to Kelly to pick up anything vital. This was textbook shock. I felt everything. I felt nothing. I was empty. I was full. All I knew was that everything felt pointless. All of it. The whole lot. I had no fight. My kite had just nose-dived from the sky.

So, my descent. This descent was now firmly in motion. No amount of childhood kite-flying could have prepared me for this fall.

If I give you each intricate and delicate moment of my cancer journey, this will need to be a bigger book. Potentially volumes. If we ever do the film version, we will be maxing out on sequels. So, I intend to bounce around a bit in order that you get the salient points. The right amount of drama. And, most importantly, the backdrop to why I wrote this book. I owe it to myself and my family to do justice to this part of the story. I want to feel back into it. And I want you to feel it too.

The hardest conversation of my life followed the next day. We called a family meeting with Mia, Mia's mum, Kelly and me. They knew. They both knew we weren't all together to tell them of a lottery win. We were there to tell Mia that her dad had cancer. 'We will treat it aggressively,' I tried to reassure her. 'We will meet it head on, with the same ferocity that it is using to circuit my body.' Mia, with her usual stillness and *less is more* ethos, sat. She just sat. She asked a couple of questions. I can't tell you what she was feeling. Maybe nothing. Maybe she was a swell of emotion. She went upstairs to her room and did what Mia does best: crank up her music and sing her heart out. We all had to deal with this adventure in the best way we could, a day at a time. There can be no one rule book for how we pilot our way through cancer. Whilst it was me who carried the illness, we all carried the emotional, psychological and physical weight of it. We were about to venture off together. And, at the same time, separately. This would be our collective journey. And our individual ones too.

For the first 2 weeks following the news, I spent most days staring out of the window. No music. No TV. No books. Just a request to be left alone with this sudden and profoundly uncomfortable meeting of my inner and outer landscape. People and the briefest of interaction were too much to carry. I was on a crashing descent without a parachute. It seemed as if nothing was catching me. We visited the hospital every day for something. Kelly took on an extra 2 jobs so that we could pay for our life. My father-in-law offered to sell his house so that we could live without the turmoil of not being able to pay our bills. Like the most violent of wildfires, this trauma was no longer contained just within me. It was consuming everything within its path. It was shared by us all. We had been chucked into a burning abyss.

We were faced with our next big decision. It seemed to be one of many on a long shopping list of things to choose. But this one somehow felt more significant. My oncologist wanted me to take a brand new drug that was in late stage trials: Obinutuzumab. It would increase my chances of getting into full molecular remission by 15%. Not to be sniffed at when you have just been told you have an incurable cancer. To have it, though, would cost us £40K. Money that we did not have. Kelly decided on a Go Fund Me campaign—it was our best shot at getting a few pennies to help towards a £40K bill. Within 6 days, we had over £40K. Sky News, newspapers and radio interviews followed. Whilst they wanted to hear the story, I was in no mood to tell it. 8.40 am and just 2 minutes before Kay Burley was about to interview me on Sky, I begged Kelly to join me. 'I don't want to do this without you.' This was our journey and I suddenly had never felt more alone. Whilst I had sought a career in the spotlight, I had hidden myself away behind characters and masks. Now all I had left was me. Bald, naked and feeling dreadfully ill. I don't know how it went. It felt like a car crash which I careered through at 90 mph. Kelly and I agreed, going forward, we come as a pair. No solos.

As the cash poured in, it did so with a flood of love, compassion and kindness. All manner of displays of support reached us. Offers to cook meals, walk the dog and testing to be a stem cell donor. Mostly, this was from people we had never met. At times, it felt almost unbearable. I had struggled for much of my life to let in love and generosity. And here I was, drowning in it.

On many occasions, I have used the term *blessed* to describe my cancer adventure. Some folks raise an eyebrow, or grimace or even snigger. It's true. I feel it. If you are going to live cancer (I see the irony in that), then let's hope it will be in a blessed way— with love, with kindness, with community. However, it struck me that whilst we may be blessed, others were not. Many people would be living their cancer adventure alone. Isolated, confused, forced to take on extra jobs when they should be resting, losing a much-needed income, travelling miles on tubes and buses for treatment. How utterly fucking terrifying. The one time when we need to be wrapped in love, it is nowhere to be seen.

It was here that The Willow Tree Foundation was brought to life. Kelly, Mia and I decided that we would set up a charity that would stand *Shoulder to Shoulder and Heart to Heart* with anyone in the UK living with a blood cancer. We'd offer grants and we'd offer practical support. Mostly, we'd stay close by. We knew that if we could channel even just a slither of some of the love that we were receiving onto others, we'd have something special.

Like any sensible person, setting up a charity when you have been given the diagnosis of a life-altering illness is, at best, questionable. At its worst, insanity. It was late on a Saturday night and I was probably high on drugs. At least that's my excuse. Who knows what Kelly's excuse was. But we both knew that establishing a firm foundation was fundamental. In some meaningful way, we could touch hearts.

Like clockwork, life arrived each day and left again, mostly leaving me in a slightly worse state than how it had found me. Lumber punctures, worries about it having spread to my central nervous system, blue-light A&E visits, PICC line cleans, vomit, blocked solid bowels, gushing displays of diarrhoea, 20 steroids a day plus a smorgasbord of other pills, prodding, poking, pulling, pushing. Every hole in my body became both an entrance and an exit. Sometimes, simultaneously. It was relentless. I remember, when I was in my teens, I'd occasionally go for afternoon tea to a posh London hotel with my mum and dad. The maître d', in all his finery, would offer us an extensive menu of food and drink. We would somehow then need to narrow down our selection to a few sandwiches and our choice of tea. My cancer journey was not dissimilar except for one standout difference: there was no maître d' and, instead, I'd be greeted by *an apron of nurses* (cool fact, huh?!) who would invite me to feast my eyes upon a wide range of oral, anal and infused drugs. Except, here, there was no choice. I'd be having them all. If I was unlucky, I'd get seconds.

Christmas arrived with as much joy as we could all muster. We donned our obligatory festive jumpers and tried to make it all as joyous as we could. With a very heavy heart, I was running my 'this could be my last Christmas' story. The only upside was that I assumed they don't wear Christmas jumpers in heaven. I know, I wasn't the guy you wanted to hang out with for fun and laughter. It all felt like a black and white movie, where the blood had been drained out.

I was mostly gifted hats. Lots of hats. Then more hats. Not just the paper kind from a cracker. Bobble, beanie, ones with ear muffs, bamboo turbans, even a knitted koala to take away the focus from the now translucent skull that was once my face. If you ever wonder what to buy a newly diagnosed cancer patient, get them a hat. And if you ever need to borrow a hat, you need only ask. As predicted, my hair started to fall out a few weeks into treatment. We were one step ahead and had shaved it all off before my Elvis quiff upped and left the building. Each day, the monster in the mirror was unrecognisable. Thank goodness for all those hats.

There are some things in life you should never have to do. One is to ask your 16-year-old daughter to shave your hair off. In all praise and admiration of Mia, she got on and did it. And did a bloody good job! If the forensic psychology path doesn't go her way, then there's always the option of being a barber.

February 7th, 2022. I had just arrived at the hospital for a 3-day inpatient stay for my chemo treatment. I have always found *treatment* to be a tough word to use in this context. I'd always taken it to mean something that happens at a spa—a mud facial, massage, waxing. For me, the clue was in the first part of the word: *treat*. Something rather magical. An unexpected experience that would bring great pleasure.

It was none of these things. Each cycle I found that bit tougher to endure than the last. This one started well. I'd hardly had time to drink my arrival tea and eat a biscuit before my oncologist called us to say that I had gotten into full remission. It was a strange, juxtaposed place. Waiting for more chemo, feeling shit.

Getting a cheery call with the good news, needing to be equally cheery in passing that news on. Realising that I now had to process remission whilst still trying to process the diagnosis. To celebrate, I could knock myself out with 3 days of toxic chemicals. Boom. The power of good news. My mother-in-law burst into tears when she was told. And she thought she might get rid of me much sooner …

Months skipped on and we prepared for my stem cell transplant. Like Cinderella as she tried on the slipper, both my siblings went through numerous tests to see if they were a perfect fit to be my donor. In this instance, less than perfect was not going to work. They weren't a fit. In fact, they were far from it. The national database had loads of *really close matches.* But the perfect one was nowhere to be found. So, my team made the decision for an autologous transplant; receiving back my own cells. These would be harvested from my body, spun fast in some snazzy sci-fi-esque centrifuge and then stuck back inside me. The few days before this happened, I got the chance for a short, luxury spa break. That is a total lie. I actually got the chance to inject my own stomach with more drugs. For 5 whole days! This was all in some vague hope that it might help me produce more cells. Oh it's the gift that keeps on giving!

It was a busy few weeks before my transplant. I worked hard to get myself in the best possible shape. I focused on my diet, some strength-building exercises and staying with my inner work. Susan, my therapist, was the most extraordinary support to me throughout. My hair grew back in some alternative colour and with a mildly frizzy pube-like texture. I walked the dog. I cooked some dinners. I took Mia to school. I laughed. I listened to music. Some days, I forgot I had cancer. Other days, I looked at my weedy white body, the pubic-hair scalp and the story the

24

physical scars told, and I wept. I was grieving my old familiar life. The life I had become attached to and expected to be there for me every day when I woke up, had been stolen. We live with such fucking privilege. We can so easily take for granted that we are blessed and fortunate to be able to breathe in life. Where had all this gone? Just a gaping chasm left. In what felt like a heartbeat, I was living in the aftermath of a chemical war.

Nothing could really prepare me for this next act of the play. I didn't believe I could descend further into the void. I'd already been body slammed and wrestled to the ground. Beaten with sticks. Left for dead. As I write this, I feel like deleting those last few sentences. I'm worried what you, my confidante, might think. *He's so dramatic.* Bit over the top isn't it? Maybe it is. Maybe that's how it will seem to you. For me, it goes some small way to revealing what this story I was living felt like. So, with my belief that life could not get any darker, it did. Yet, hidden amongst the jet-black days, there were flickers of light. They were faint, but they were there. It was, however, the darkness that, like a leech, was eating away at me.

May 3rd was admission day. Rebirth was on the horizon. Now, Kelly doesn't cry very often. Today she did. We had to say our farewells at the entrance to The Ruth Myles Ward, St George's Hospital, Tooting. She wasn't even allowed to come to my penthouse suite to help me unpack. It's a highly sanitised area and whilst Kelly had a shower that very morning, no amount of washing gets you entry. Unless you are going there to have a full oil change. This was my purpose. Our final hug felt frighteningly final. Most people make it out of their SCT alive. Some don't. 'What if' scenarios weighed heavy.

I settled into my 8ft × 7ft white room. The first treatment they offered me was to have a central line placed into my chest so that

I could be given all manner of drugs and goodies. This was …
mighty bloody painful. Day 2 followed and then Day 3 and then
4 … and so it went on. I don't know who booked me into this
spa, but the treatments went downhill by the day. Most of them
ended with some form of bodily eruption; either in the guise of
vomit or shit.

Then it was Melphalan Day. You could be confused into
thinking this is some kind of mystical day to celebrate the Greek
god Melphalan. But no. Melphalan is the somewhat infamous
highlight of most SCTs. A chemo drug infusion that burns
your mucosa from your mouth, right down to your arsehole.
The solution? Cram every last space in your body with ice; ice
cream, ice pops, ice cubes and, if there's room, an igloo. I did
this for a full 7 hours, constant. Don't ever offer me a Calippo.
Over the coming days, the burning of my mouth and throat
was something else. Even the syringe driver of Oxycodone that
was nailed to my thigh failed to take the pain away. Some things
cannot be put into words. It hurt me. It really hurt me. A lot.

I hit my lowest point around this time. My body and soul
were wracked with pain. I took medication designed to soothe
the torture that didn't seem to touch the sides. I woke up during
one rather memorable night, dreaming that I'd shit myself.
But when I felt around amongst the sheets, it was clear that
despite what my mum had told me as I grew up, dreams do
actually come true. I had. It was everywhere. At the same time,
my hair had decided to pack its bags and leave again. Not only
was I rolling in my own wet faeces, I was looking at my white
pillow turned black. I couldn't get my pyjamas off. I was still
attached to a drug line. I was tripping out from the Oxycodone.
Yet I desperately needed to wash myself before enduring the
humiliation of telling the nurses what I'd done.

I had a go with the shower, only to find how drenched I was in poo and hair. It was all hopeless. The crippling shame I felt stopped me from pressing my emergency buzzer. I wanted to fix this one by myself. However, sometimes, no amount of will can fix us when we are broken. And in this moment, I was broken. Like burnt caramel shattered into splinters. I. Was. Broken. I crumbled—emotionally, physically, psychologically. It was as if I were washing myself down the plughole, yet the poo and the hair remained present, refusing to leave. I pressed the bell. The nurses were, of course, bright, breezy and got on with cleaning up me and my room. I still bear the scars from this night. It was weeks before I even told Kelly. On many occasions during the writing of this book, I deleted this sequence. Then added it back in again. I ping-ponged between sharing this dark and deeply personal secret with you and keeping it locked away in my own basement. With the hope that you will become more discerning about what you lock away and what you let go of, I chose to keep it in.

On May 10th, 2022, I was reborn. It is called your Re-Birth-Day. It's like the hard drive is wiped and a new operating system is installed. All childhood inoculations eradicated too. I wanted so desperately to bounce up from this darkness and into the light. I knew it would be bad but this was all far harder than I'd imagined. Much harder. As I write this, months on, it's still all very alive in me. When I listen to people speak of their most heartbreaking tales of despair and descent, I sometimes cannot imagine having enough empathy in me to understand. And then I'm reminded that actually, I do. I have, in my own way, waded around in the waist-deep, sticky, toxic, shit of life.

So, where am I now? Well, NDY. Not Dead Yet. It became a family joke on the day I found out my most recent PET scan was clear. Occasionally you have to gift yourself a laugh as you hurtle down towards the abyss. Right now I live with an invisible disability. People meet me and tell me how fabulous I am looking. A full head of hair, stubble on my face and not a whiff of lymphoma. That *they* can see. I can see it. In fact, only I see it. Whilst Kelly, Mia and Royston, my fluffy son, are only too aware of my energy ups and downs and the aftermath of life with a rock-bottom immunity, they cannot possibly see the cracks that run within. Each one, a deep ravine leading into the large underground pool of molten rock sitting at my core.

As a result of platinum-based chemotherapy drugs, I have tinnitus in both ears and a significant reduction in my hearing: 65% less in one ear and 30% less in the other. My peripheral neuropathy in both feet is shocking. It leaves me with pain in the balls of each foot along with a numbness. Will they recover? Who knows. I am told by mainstream medicine, No. We are hunting around for whatever intervention can support my healing and alleviate the symptoms. Throughout this adventure, we have included integrative therapies as well as an orthodox approach. My mood is consistently inconsistent. Some days the world looks rosy, other days it looks fucked. I have 3 years of Rituximab maintenance treatment ahead of me. This seems to batter my immunity so I'm left with coughs and upper respiratory infections that outstay their welcome. Oh, and then add in an incurable lymphoma that we live, day to day, trying to hold back from visiting us again.

As I said, most of this remains unseen and not understood by others. It's barely understood by me. If you are reading this book and live with an invisible illness yourself, such as chronic fatigue, endometriosis, arthritis, Crohn's disease, mental conditions etc., you can relate. But unless you have lived experience of a life-altering illness, you cannot comprehend the enormous burden. It's quite simply impossible for any of us to truly make sense of the load others carry. It is hard enough making sense of the load that I lug around. I'm not playing victim. This is currently how it feels to be me. Later on, I may feel better. Or worse. I just can't call it.

What is clear for me, though, is this. I won't mask up just to play to my audience. I have done that before and whilst it is the most familiar role to me in my life, it also comes with the greatest cost. I want to live from the most truthful place I can. I hope to keep myself honest. Whilst cancer has taken away from my life, it has also handed me a new lifeline.

These months since diagnosis have gifted me many hours to ponder various questions. Is this it? What else? How could my life make my heart dance? What exactly is Richard Tyler in this cosmos for? How can I leave our planet ever so slightly better than I found it? The answers exist. Whilst I can stand on my timeline of 51 years and look to the future for the answers in hope that I can figure it out, my heart knows that what I need most exists in the other direction. At *home*. Going back to the source. Travelling back to my truest nature and form. BUT. Facing forwards on the train, not facing away. I have been handed the chance to reconnect with my Self. My soul. Whilst soul choreographs our destiny, our personality wants to steer a different route.

When, during our life, we stray so far away from our home, we will most likely get lost. We abandon our essence so that we can best play this game of being human. From here on in, I pledge to wind my way homeward bound. It is from this point that I am committing to be the hero of my own quest. To journey back through the numerous masks and costumes that have been donned during my life, in hope that I can better boogie between the dark and the light.

Whether I like it or not, I have set out on my pilgrimage home.

Four

With my life's foundation firmly planted in singing, music and theatre, I am often asked what it is I think that makes the difference between those musicians who are perhaps more *ordinary* in their playing and those who excel at being *extraordinary*. There are of course many individual qualities that could play into this distinction, too many to comment on or even comprehend. And yet I continue to be drawn back to one quality in particular. The rest. The pause. The space.

Maybe we start by acknowledging what is common between them both: the number of notes they can play. Musical notes are musical notes. In many Eastern cultures, they use different scales to the ones familiar in the West. If you choose to listen with your whole body, you will hear a richer cacophony of sound. The Eastern musician is bestowed with an abundance of notes to play and sing above and beyond our Western harmonics. But, ultimately, a musical note is a musical note. The ordinary and the extraordinary, then, begin at the very same starting block. So, what does determine someone who is an extraordinary player over someone who is a more ordinary player? My view is that the spaces in between each note are what makes the greatest difference.

The rest. The silence. That short, or extended, moment where the world comes to a halt and the earth's all-hearing sense wonders what choice will be made next. It is *these* moments where some musicians step into a different league. It is in this space that they breathe in their audience, the mood, the ambience of the room, the story they are telling, their internal state and the wealth of feelings that dance and swirl around. Discernment. Choice. Wisdom. All wonderfully entwined and dancing together. This isn't about following what the dots on the paper indicate should be played next. No, this is about absorbing what it means to be alive in this very beat of life. Whilst the dots offer up a map, they are not the territory. They are merely a suggestion as to what could come next. This space offers the musical storyteller a choice. And it is here that we come to discover that the music lives *between* the notes and is not just the notes themselves.

In stand-up comedy we might call it *comedic timing*. For an actor, it's holding the tension of the *dramatic pause*. In graphic design, it is the *white space*. In music, it's *a rest*. Each one giving spaciousness. A pregnant pause where we wait for the birthing process to begin, knowing it can only happen when the gestation cycle is complete. In each medium, these spaces are designed to strengthen the energies at play between the artist and their audience.

If we track a path right back to indigenous tribes, they held great importance in the oral traditions and that of storytelling. Holding silence allowed reconnection and would deepen the interplay between the story, the orator and the listener. In Japanese, they have a word that we simply do not have in our English language: *Ma*, meaning the silence before the sound. The audience waits with curious anticipation as to what might come next. This space, the silence, is not a void, but an entity filled with energy and purpose. Mystery surrounds this moment in the telling of the story. The story doesn't cease in the silence. In fact, quite the contrary. It is here that the story intensifies and

31

deepens. As an actor, I would play a game with myself to see for just how long I could tenderly cup this journey between what passed and what was in sight. Always doing my best to sense, when it felt too long, what effect it might have on the audience and the narrative at play.

The arts have certainly known this for millennia. Many of our spiritual traditions, too, have embodied this sense of space and presence: Buddhism, Zen, Daoism, Sufism. Yet here we are, living in a world which drowns us in knowledge, noise, sound, words, colours, pictures and notes. So many notes. And without the spaces in between. A dissonance of opinions and views and dictates that suffocate us. The rhythms are haphazard. Contrary motions of jangling melodies confront us. We seem to be living in a maze of minor keys and open-ended cadences. We move chromatically, step by step. The array of discord tests us. We are left searching for resolution. I often feel held hostage by the overwhelm of information, from mostly well-meaning people, who clearly seem to know what I *should* be doing next. I fight to catch my breath but as I come up for air, I am bombarded with more. We have become immune to the din. It's now normal for us. *Ma* is simply a beautiful word from Japan that remains a construct rather than a reality.

These past months have, for me, been a time of stripping back. A year of simplification. An expanse for me to marinate in less, rather than more. A reduction of my outer landscape which permitted me to be discerning about what I hold in my inner landscape. When too much stuff weighs the kite down, it will simply not fly. My kite was grounded. If you observed MLBC—My Life Before Cancer—you'd see how I was a slave to the notes. Endlessly drawn into a musical battle that I was never going to be triumphant in. What would have been spaces had more notes squeezed in, making the most of time. Just in case. After all, you never know what life might throw at you, so best not to waste a beat.

After 50 years of filling my life up, I have now decided to empty out. I want less clutter. And more space.

One of my deep hopes for this book (I have a few) is that it will offer you some moments of spaciousness and pause too. How rarely we do this—pause, breathe, reflect. For anything to ripen and mature, we must grant it time, space and the optimum conditions. Ripening is a highly complex process that involves thousands of micro adaptations and developments. If we rush through, we simply eat the inedible. Insights, intuitions, encounters, and dreams, all require time to incubate and consolidate into something substantial. Therefore, I have resisted cramming these pages with words and maxing out on chapter numbers.

One of the characters I hold inside me is The King of Shoulds. Nice bloke. Bit pushy. Keeps trying to barge in and tell me what I *should* think, *should* feel and *should* do next. He believes that every reader wants maximum value, word count and pages. I also have an inner rebel who tells him to go fuck himself and tells me to write the story that my heart wants to speak. It is from his counsel that I have decided I am not going to follow the dots on the page just because it's expected. I am aiming for optimal value and, at the same time, will be culling words.

The reality for me is that I don't actually know why you are reading this book. Maybe you found a copy lying on a train. Or picked it up on eBay, cheap. Perhaps it leapt off the shelf in a bookshop or a friend bought it for you. I assume, though, that there was some slither of curiosity. It looks and feels different and maybe it brushes gently across a nerve. I have no clue as to your personal reasoning for getting this far through. Maybe your life is also filled with an endless Spotify playlist of notes, yours and others. And perhaps you, like me, crave some spaces in between.

The magnitude of this year has left me sharply scarred. Not all the scar tissue has formed yet, so more will be revealed over the coming years. For now, I am only too well aware of the rupture my body feels. I'm shredded. Some days are easier than others and it's as if I glide through, hardly recalling the viciousness of the past months. Other days, I hover above myself and see the 1,000-piece jigsaw of my existence, scattered across the floor. I see the corners of my inner landscape where my anxiety and depressed state lay their weary heart.

One of the benefits of my crazy strong painkillers is that they help elevate my mood and blot out the enormous sense of loss I feel. Whilst I acknowledge the need for the strong drugs to start exiting stage left, I know that some days it is only by allowing them to remain on stage that I can cope. A thin veil exists between my hope and my despair. This book is one of the ways in which I stand shoulder to shoulder with myself. *As a Kite Falls* is helping to prop me up by encouraging me to walk the inner terrain of my life. I've donned my boots and I am ready to get muddy. I come armed with a torch which might help me when the darkness overwhelms. And I have a hot-water bottle as, since this illness began, the cold brutalises my skeleton. The fact that you are reading this is a bonus. I'm not used to doing much for me. This book, though, is just that. It's for me. It is my way of illuminating my own story so that I can heal, better understand and go some way towards *repairenting* myself.

Childhood bedtimes would often involve me snuggling under the duvet with my copy of Heaney and Hughes' edited anthology, *The Rattle Bag*. No mugging old people for me when dusk fell.

It was all poems, a mug of tea and a digestive biscuit. To this day, it remains a stable part of my childhood baptism into theatre and storytelling.

As a Kite Falls is certainly no rattly bag of poems! I have chosen haiku to help me tell my story. Actually, they chose me. Until I lay in my hospital bed for 4 weeks having a transplant, I had never heard of them. I still cannot quite remember how I even got to read one—maybe it was on a card or tucked inside one of the library of books I was gifted. Anyway, it was love at first reading. I remember being struck by their simplicity, beauty and profound essence. They are wonderfully neat and I like that. They have a simple structure. Often, life inside my head can be overwhelming and noisy. These short poems hold me to something more compact and tidy. They say everything. And they say nothing.

Haiku are Japanese short-form poetry. Traditional, structured and usually unrhyming, they are well known for the rule of 5/7/5: five syllables in the first line, seven in the second, and five again in the third. In 17th century Japan, Matsuo Bashō adopted them as his hallmark style whilst studying Zen philosophy. He believed the haiku was an opportunity to compress the meaning of the world into a simple pattern, leaving glimmers of hope in small, simple things and revealing the connectedness of all life on earth.

Today, haiku are no longer limited to the subject of nature, although nature is still a popular topic. Haiku can be written for anything. There are haiku to make you laugh, to raise social awareness, to evoke emotion and to reminisce on the past. The idea of compression though, remains the same. Haiku are a microcosm of a larger idea or feeling. They give me what I need; a way to express myself with brevity and discernment. They remind us that all things express themselves through form. A wild rose has five petals. The heart has four chambers. The primary colours, three in number, combine to make all of the rest. There is infinite variety in the natural world, but all of it fits into the greater pattern of the whole.

Haiku offer poignant glimpses into my own life and the collective life we are a part of. Small shards of truth: 17 syllables that support us to cut away the undergrowth and weeds that so often prevent us from cultivating change and assigning meaning to our over-complicated time on earth. I value the order that they give me. I can be creative, knowing that the form will hold my thoughts, firmly. I relish being able to describe my inner scenery in a handful of syllables. From the chaos of my mind comes order. This relentless yearning for more has exhausted me. None of us need look too far to find a world that has been decimated and much of what remains are the scars of exhaustion, burnout and overwhelm.

I wonder if less can give us more. A better way. A simpler guide to wandering our path. One that is less cluttered and holds greater potential and much less suffocation. Haiku cannot fix the problems associated with our busy minds. The busyness may well continue, but the practice of writing them can both help to simplify and gain clarity. They are, maybe, a route through to our practising the art of *enoughness.*

Contained within the subsequent chapters, you will find each haiku planted firmly in the centre of white space. Don't be tricked into thinking that the wisdom and the insight are found only in the words. Their tendrils are to be found as much in the spaces as they are in the words themselves. On the following page I have gently placed where the haiku was birthed into my existence. I felt it was important to offer some reflections that led me to capture my experience in just 17 syllables. I hope this context will help in your reflections as you gather meaning which can be applied to your own path in life.

This year has brought me back into relationship with the natural world. I find myself deepening my relationship with Mother Earth and all whom she holds. I have a newfound reverence for our seasons. They reveal a rhythm that we have, perhaps, due to the frenetic desire for ascent, lost. Each season crosses a threshold into the next. We are offered a moment to pause. But do we take it? We cannot bring about long summer days until we have lived through the autumn, winter and spring that lay the ground for the many summer riches. For the buds of spring to arrive, we must first travel through winter. But sometimes, I am left wondering if we try to be cleverer than our natural world. *I want summer, now. Give me summer. Give me those strawberries in December!* It's a little like Violet Beauregarde from *Charlie and the Chocolate Factory*. Her persistent whining and greed for more turned her into a blueberry. Too often, we act like plump blueberries. Waddling around, ready to explode and yet still wanting more. We chase the destination and we want it on our terms, failing to notice the impact and often missing the point that the natural rhythm of life, just outside the window, is our perfect guide.

If only we could dare ourselves to listen and to then hear. I have nature all around me. And at the same time, I am nature. It rests within me. I am both the acorn and the oak tree. My soul, the truest essence of who I am, knows all this. It's just that my life here as Richard has forgotten it all. Coming face to face with my own mortality this past year has brought it back into extremely sharp focus. As the seasons know how to pause, so do I. As nature in all its wisdom knows how to pause, so do I.

Much of my voyage through descent has been unbearable. Such darkness that I had no way of holding. This continues. Some days I feel as if I can't even catch my breath. But when I step outside and renew my relationship with Mother Earth once more, I remember how nothing is too much for her to hold. She carries all that I cannot. It is amongst the beauty of nature that I have found a new practice …

As I scratched my head, wondering how the heck I order the haiku in this book, I settled on the notion of seasonality. You will find each one sits elegantly within a season. This allows both you and I to walk through my story chronologically and, at the same time, get back in sync with the cycles and the earth's natural beat. Of course, as is the case for most of us, each season brings us 4 seasons in 1. They are fluid and, as our climate changes, so does the predictable rhythm that seasons once assured us of. You will find my dark winter included glimmers of spring bud and summer bloom. This adventure with lymphoma stripped me back to my complete nakedness, so it seems only right to start the seasons with winter. I feel like this season in particular reveals all truths, as did my cancer.

Ultimately, *As a Kite Falls* is somewhere that you can lay down your luggage and rest a while as you venture through your own liminal space. It is, if you like, your bench. Use it as your own place to dwell. I have vivid memories of being aged 5 in Mrs King's class. She was mostly hair. Potentially housing a tiny nest of sparrows. Backcombed. She was about 5 ft. Her hair added an additional 2 ft. Mrs King could have been a character in a Roald Dahl story if she hadn't ended up being a teacher. I have a vivid recollection of how she would crouch down next to me when I felt stuck or anxious. The gentle fluttering of wings could be heard from deep within her course black hair. Her warm eyes, reaching mine. She met me where I was. Her beautiful big heart was willing to hold everything that I couldn't. However difficult a place I was lost in, she would always find me. I have ventured through life wanting to bring the same quality to bear for others. I've longed to be one of those souls who will crouch down next to another and give my unconditional presence. Regardless of how difficult a place they may find themselves in, I endeavour to meet them there. Thank you, Mrs King. I may not have left with the gift of an 11+ gold star, but I left with a value that is unshakable in my life. I am under no illusion that my imbalance of crouching down next to others throughout my life has contributed to my own descent into ill health. It is now a time when my soul is calling me to recalibrate, adjust and rebalance. So, this past year has been about practising the art of crouching down next to myself. Loving me, without conditions. I have learnt that this is my life's work. Do the work on yourself and you can do the work on the world. So, here I am. Discovering all manner of ways to do my own work, one of which is writing *my* story that I feel compelled to share.

I don't know where this book will lead you. I have no idea what flames it might ignite and what fires it might extinguish. I wonder if, as we voyage together, you might consider how your own life experiences might feel if they were bathed in *Ma*. Among the many spaces between the notes, I am unsure where you will ascend. I imagine it will bring about some scurries into descent too. After all, if we are to go up, we must be open to going down. We have both. We need both.

So, I'm inviting you to get close and take a personal peek into the route that I took. It's not *the* truth though. It's my truth. *The* truth doesn't exist. I hope all that I share will encourage you to find your way into your own spaces, so, rather than being driven by both the fear of descent and hope for ascent, you can *bench yourself* in the here and now. Amongst all of the light and all of the dark that you discover whilst reading this book, I can assure you of one thing: I will be walking alongside. And in the moments that you fall and find yourself wanting someone to crouch down beside you, I will meet you there. My wish for you is that, in time, you will make the space to meet yourself, wherever you may be, comforted by your own wisdom to trust that as your kite may fall, so it will rise again.

WINTER

enso: the Japanese word that reminds us that immense beauty is to be found in imperfection—it shows how the circle of life, connection and unity, are of the utmost importance to human existence

As winter reveals itself, we start to see the berries shining red on the holly bush. The last of the sloes waving goodbye to yet another year. The trees stand naked. The birds, no longer hidden, flit from branch to branch. The oak bears its final few leaves. The shrill summer sound of the lawnmower ends as it is laid to rest for another season. The very first snowdrops are peeking through, winking at us. Native primroses and their pretty yellow blooms hide amongst ancient hedgerows. Amorous foxes screech and bark their way through the night. Robins chirping their silvery song. The tawny owl reminds predators that this is his patch. Starlings take to the skies for their annual aerial displays. Dormice, hedgehogs and bats remain deep in slumber. Much of our natural world takes the opportunity to strip back, yawn and take its rest.

For us humans navigating this season, it is perhaps also a time for snuggling down and finding the space for our deep rest; for hibernation. Winter is a time for us to enjoy solitude, to dream and contemplate. It is our placeholder where we can amass energy, to restore and repair. Drawn to hot soups and plates of comforting carbs, we satisfy our bellies with rich goodness. Nights are spent hunkered down watching old movies. The first sprinkling of snow helps to slow our system down. Our tiredness from a summer spent focused on the beauty around us beckons us to go inside to soothe mind and body. As the year draws to a close, the many festivities of this time afford us moments to mark out endings. These winter months, a liminal space, offer us the opportunity to reflect on what was: our learning, our insights and our wisdom. It is not a place for new ideas. That time will come soon enough.

Winter is patient with us. After all, it's not leaving anytime soon. We cannot rush through this.

And so began my own wintering. A profound coldness that burnt me to my bones. All that I looked at felt utterly hopeless.

---

you stand within me
poised to pounce and lead me off
my time is not done

I mean, if I was going to shack up with any cancer, it would of course have to be one that likes the idea of returning to pounce on me. Why didn't I get something a little more straightforward, even predictable. But no, I have Mantle Cell Lymphoma. Until only a few years ago, the life expectancy was 3–5 years. Treatments have evolved at a breathtaking rate and the odds now fare much better. And, I believe, by owning my destiny with as much control as I can through the use of various integrative approaches, I will have the maximum time here on Planet Earth that I possibly can. Orthodox medicine gives us only so much. It does not hold all the answers. I digress. My reality is that I have a cancer that is considered incurable. I can remain in remission for many years to come and I will still have MCL.

I've had a recurring dream. Sometimes whilst I sleep and often when I am awake. It's juxtaposed, so stay with me. One part of the image is the archetypal grim reaper; black hooded cloak, faceless, chilling, a raised hand that grasps a scythe, tall, very tall, still, intimidating. He remains poised. Me, frozen to the spot. But then I feel a warmth emanate from him. He pulls me in. It feels like … kindness, yes, kindness. And all of a sudden the terror I felt drains and I am filled to the brim with love. The end. For many of the early months, this played on repeat. Now, less so. But I am still aware of it.

The grim reaper and kindness should not really go together. But for me, they do. I often wonder about this. Deep down I feel that the grim reaper's presence is there to startle me and grab my attention. He reminds me to stay truthful. He shows me that only a slither of space exists between my life and my death. He jolts me to stay awake and conscious. No more sleepwalking. The kindness? Well, I see this as his way of revealing how his intention for me is good. I might not like it, but he means well. His role is one of service.

How often is this the case for us, but we just don't see it because we are handcuffed to our own fears? We find ourselves on a path of descent and our ability to see is suddenly compromised. We are plunged into darkness or we choose to look away. But I am left wondering: what if descent held an intention for our life that was in fact positive? How might we then walk that path with a renewed energy and focus?

the edge beckoned me
but it was your final push
that shattered my world

I'm not stupid. Neither would I label myself as super smart. But I do believe I possess a superpower: attunement. It's a quality that I take huge pride in living. It's a much-needed and underrated quality that our planet is begging us to bring more of.

It is this superpower that allowed me to tune into the feeling that something within my body was desperate to get my attention. I knew I was ill. I knew that something bad was hurtling towards me. In my best moments, I was able to look away, squint and pretend I couldn't see it. But, I knew. I was being pulled towards the edge and with all the might I could muster, I stood firmly in resistance.

Until, that is, I met Dr Pettengell. In our first 3 hours together, she blew my entire world into smithereens. She stood next to me, right on the very edge. As I exhaled, she pushed. 'You have a rare lymphoma, Mantle Cell. Only a few hundred people in the UK each year get it. It's stage 4b.' My listening ground to a halt. I'd heard quite enough. My attunement plug, that kept me tethered to the outside world, was ripped out.

This meeting, this date, this moment, remain profoundly etched into my heart. It is when everything changed, forever.

Through it all, my attunement has been unwavering. There's a telling difference though. Whereas it had historically been focused on my outer landscape, it is now in its infancy with how it works to protect and parent my inner landscape. It really is a superpower. It really is saving my life. It's a superpower that we can all embody. You too. No cape required.

---◆---

**hope is everything
hold yours with such tenderness
it will hold you too**

---◆---

What is radical hope? I see radical hope as being the grace that comes once we hit rock bottom. Radical hope demands courage.

I remember writing this haiku. I sat on my bed, asking myself if this hospital stay would ever end. I had just lived through the worst night on record and wondered if I had left all hope behind me, and entered a place of pure despair. Hope, literally, dangled on a thread. The last drop of hope that was left in me needed to be handled with enormous love and tenderness. Deep down I knew this. Yet gifting tenderness onto my own body was unfamiliar. Who had ever shown me this? If I had not felt it, how could I offer it to myself?

I see hope as being an embrace of the unknown and the unknowable. It is a sure alternative to the certainty of both optimism and pessimism. It locates itself within the premise that we simply don't know what will happen. And within that space is the room to take action. Whilst my cancer required a gargantuan effort, we did our best to become consistent action takers.

Something told me that if I were to slow right down, hope would hold me and I wouldn't have to grapple with despair. Well, I'm still here. Holding space for hope to exist. Not just the radical hope I hold for myself, but the radical hope that I hold for our planet and for each of its inhabitants.

---◆---

smile for the camera
if only they knew the truth
scolded and then shamed

---◆---

I was 5 weeks into my treatment. I felt as ill as I now looked; gaunt, translucent, hairless, weak. We got a call one afternoon from a PR agency to say that Kay Burley from Sky News would like to do a breakfast-show TV interview with us. It was to talk about the fundraising and the charity. It would be early the following day.

I propped myself up with cushions. Checked to make sure my eyebrows were straight (no hair but, somehow, the eyebrows stayed). And then I found out that the interview was going to be just me, flying solo. No Kelly. No *us*. They wanted to speak with me only. Half my soul was peeled away. I could have burst into tears like a toddler who'd just had his favourite comforter snatched. A Sky News meltdown was not how I wanted to be remembered in this lifetime.

The masks we wear, the armour we don, all in an attempt to hide ourselves away. Early life experiences teach us the importance of this as being an intelligent and wise method of survival. As we hide, so we build our protective fortress. We tell one story to the world and yet, inside, a different narrative grips us. At some junction in our lives, these stories, these masks, these sturdy walls, begin to crumble away. Our truths revealed.

I was a mass of contradiction. My attempt to sound upbeat, was simply the mask that I hoped would hide the deep shame

I felt. I was the new Quasimodo: desperate to be loved but knowing I was so very ugly. Only I knew this truth. I clothed my fakery in a story that might just appeal to the masses. What hurt me the most was that this was bitterly familiar. I had been here before. Too many times.

she smiles right at me
tricking the drab room into
believing it's ok

I've pondered for a while as to who *she* is. My mum? My feminine aspect? Soul? My Self? Her smile reached right in, caressing my heart. She exuded warmth. To be honest, the single, small, drab white room I was in did not feel that ok. In fact, it felt unsafe. Unstable. I felt unstable. But somehow, *she* offered me some hope; some comfort and a degree of reassurance. It felt like a maternal quality. Her smile was tender and oozed love. Like Mrs King, she crouched down next to me. I believe that there is no greater gift we can offer another than that of our unconditional presence.

Eastern traditions speak to the idea of our masculine and feminine energies: Shiva and Shakti. These divine energies live within us all and we each have masculine and feminine aspects to our being. The idea is that when these two aspects come into balance and unite, our system can settle. I have always lived with a dominance of Shakti energy (feminine). These qualities are about kindness, compassion, creativity, being gentle and tender. Each aspect requires the opposite in order to be most present and mature. My feminine energies have consistently, across my life, been gifted to others. I have missed out on gifting them to myself.

The question remains: who is she? Perhaps, at the time in my life when I needed it most, I was offering love and tenderness to my Self.

haiku are simple
the first two lines are a breeze
but then i fuck it up with some elongated
third line that trashes the rest

Sometimes, I laugh at my jokes. I know, it's not a good trait. But this one is funny! I can talk incessantly about how the form of haiku holds me tight and ensures I remain focused on mining the kernels of truth.

But sometimes, I want to stick 2 fingers up and be a rebel. I know what you're thinking: this is me being a rebel?! Errrrrrr … yeah. Form is reliable. It brings consistency and order. It can help tether us when we come across chaos. Form is predictable.

As I have journeyed through this descent, there have been many times I have wanted and needed to be a rebel. Breaking the norms has allowed me to ensure I can support myself when I felt like those around me were not working in my best interests. I have always needed to be better at this. All too often in life I have found myself saying 'ok' when, frankly, the system, the relationship or the form, were not serving me and it was therefore only me who was going to shift the trajectory.

Poetry is about breaking rules. Innovation is about breaking rules. Being with descent means breaking some rules.

What rules keep you bound? Where do they confine and restrict you? Where is form keeping you held prisoner?

As Charlie Parker so eloquently put it, 'Master your instrument, Master the music, and then forget all that bullshit and just play.'

there's much i don't have
focusing on it too long
taints all that i have

A theft had occurred. I felt like I was being robbed of all that I had. Not just the physical (strength, flexibility, hair) and the tangible (money, time, theatre trips) but the emotional and psychological too (pride, faith, confidence).

Most self-help books pedal the story of focusing on gratitude. I'd pedalled it too in both my writing, online videos and talks. But bringing it into being and making it something more than just an exercise grounded in a *should* is a stretch. And doing it when your life is so broken, feels nigh on impossible.

I'm not talking about going for a picnic and, even though it pours with rain, thunders and a cow eats your scones, you still look on the bright side … No, I'm speaking of true gratitude for life and all that it bestows on us. I mean a life where we appreciate all that is available, even when we cannot quite grasp it. I'm talking about leaning in, full of reverence and appreciation.

During the peak of my illness, some days were dire. No, most days. Sorting through, hunting out anything that resembles shiny, has often felt utterly pointless. And yet, it is in our hours of darkness that we need to most acknowledge the faintest glimmer of light.

when the lights go out
feel your way through the darkness
or just get a torch

And just like that, my world was plunged into darkness. Winter had smothered me. The first few weeks, post-diagnosis, were some of the toughest I have known. It was as if I couldn't locate anything. I reached out, fumbled around, but it wasn't there.

One of my strongest childhood memories is of fearing the dark when I was in bed. Our landing light was on a dimmer. No sooner had my mum or dad wished me goodnight, they would be out in the hallway, turning it down. I'd wait. Then, sensing the moment that the 9 o'clock news jingle was in full swing, I would tiptoe to the hallway, avoiding the obstacles en route, reaching my destination and slowly turning the dimmer up. Like the hero in the film, delicately turning the dial so as not to blow up the ticking bomb. In an instant, my world settled. The additional brightness somehow allowed my inner terrain to become clearer. Peace. And then my dad would march up the stairs like the Grand Old Duke of York and turn it right down. This game could go on for hours. My heart literally shook with anxiety amongst the fragments of darkness. Eventually my eyes would adjust. But how could I bear the burden of that bitterly dark moment. A liminal space between what was and what might be. I was terrified of feeling lost and therefore *unfindable* (made-up word alert).

The beautiful poem by David Wagoner, *Lost*, never fails to bring me comfort. *Lost,* reminds us that we must 'Stand Still. The forest knows where you are. You must let it find you'.

Forty years later, the same strange terror of being lost and unfindable had taken me hostage again. Even the torch was of no help. I waited. And stood still. Trying to remain hopeful that I would eventually be found.

i hide and you seek
i'll go where you can't find me
cowered from the world

I do appreciate how, for so many people, they wanted to *find me* in those first few long weeks following diagnosis day. Finding me took many guises; gifting love, seeing how I was feeling, offering support and generally checking that I was doing ok. But I wasn't doing ok. Why the hell would I be doing ok? Each time they moved towards me, I burrowed deeper. There was nothing they could offer me that would make any of this ok. Nothing.

I sound like a jumped-up brat. But I had never in my life faced something such as this. Every aspect of it was bleak. I had no answers. I had no voice. I had nothing to say and everything to say. The only thing I wanted was to hide. I can't honestly say that I wanted to be well again at this stage. It was as if my system shut down. It was overloaded and made the best choice it could: hide and switch off.

It's impossible to know how to best respond when someone is given such a life-altering diagnosis. Until we have lived it ourselves, how could we imagine what someone else might need? I don't recall any part of my education that taught me how to be with my own grief, and that of others. Having cancer has taught me that rather than being in a position where I offer my love and support when the person desperately cries out for it, I need to ensure the people in my life know how much they matter all of the time. Why wait until someone is already hurtling into descent. Catch them sooner. Much sooner. Find them whilst they aren't hiding.

i long for release
from my journey homeward bound
this is not freedom

I remember this particular Wednesday fairly well. The previous week, I'd had a 3-day chemo cycle. These generally seemed to beat and batter my body. On this day, I was feeling the aftermath of a system crammed full of toxins. Soon after waking, I'd entered into some kind of a dogfight with my morning pills. I almost didn't win. The pills sought victory and fought hard. But I did it. One pill. One sip. And on to the next.

Life felt like one brawl after another. Kelly congratulated me on my pill-taking and reminded me that we did still need to get to the hospital for my weekly PICC line flush, obs and some ceremonial bloodletting. Here I was, barely able to lift my head. Placing just one inward breath after the effort of an exhale left me ready to sob. In the enormous void between breaths I questioned my resolve to carry on. Did I have anything left to give? Was I *man enough to tough it out*? I didn't ask for this fucking illness to take such a grip on me. Who did it think it was, barging in here and taking me hostage. This was no life. There was no bliss in this. It was joyless. And I was empty. I had been mugged and my freedoms of being human robbed from me.

In order to *be* in life, we need to be *home*. We are, after all is said and done, each making our journey home. We simply don't know when we will arrive. I had dreamt of walking the way of beauty to get there. But instead, had been dragged into some macabre alternative reality. The laughter that had surrounded funny hats for Christmas, bald heads and jokes about needing to draw on eyebrows, had passed. I. Wanted. Out.

once more we begin
to paint our fresh new canvas
waiting for your art

Dear 2021

Thank you for gifting me an utter shitshow. I had not set out with the intention of picking up some stage-4 cancer. But you ensured that I did.

Thank you for mugging me and stealing my life.

Yours truly
Richard

Hello 2022 … Happy New Year to you!

*I am not sure if you have been in touch with 2021 or if, like our UK government agencies, you work independently and have no communication channels. Anyway, 2021 was a bit tricky for me and my family. So, I was wondering if I could request a few things for this coming year. Thank you for dropping off the new blank canvas. And the selection of brushes and some paints was a bonus. I am wondering whether or not to paint something that represents what I want more of. Something literal. Then, in true adult style, I can berate and shame myself for being such a hopeless artist. I can then spend the next 12 months trying to make it as perfect a painting as I can. The experience of doing it will be a little stressful. And totally joyless, as I attempt to navigate the voice of my art teacher who always told me my drawings were hilarious and **like I'd done it with my eyes closed!***

Or. I could paint it like I have the will, enthusiasm and complete lack of attachment or expectation that a 3-year-old has when you give them a blank canvas and some paints. I understand that you may not recognise what I paint. But frankly, I will have such a bloody brilliant time doing it, I don't care. My heart will overflow with joy. Every fibre in my body will be doing the bolero. And crafting my 2022 will be a ball of delight.

Yep. I've decided. I'm going to enjoy this canvas-painting lark. Like my year ahead, I will be filled with as much deep play and joy as I can summon up.

See you on the other side. Actually, I have cancer so I might not. But I'll do my best.

With love and gratitude
Rich

———◆———

How do you approach the blanks canvases in your life?

With the adult mind?

Or your beginner's mind?!

you steal my silence
robbing me of my right to
peace and solitude

I love sound: birdsong, voices, the wind, waves that crash against each other like bumper cars, an overture, a drink being poured over ice, sublime musicianship. Sounds matter to me and I am grateful to have spent much of my life being able to tune in and then tune out. I suppose I could be found guilty of taking it for granted.

In the many months before my diagnosis, I was starting to find various sounds grating: voices, TV, loud music that I hadn't chosen. Maybe I can group these sounds as artificial. I wanted to drown my ears in sounds only from the natural world.

Earlier in the book I spoke of *Ma: the silence before the sound.* And the importance of *spaces between the notes.* My yearning for silence was building. I enjoyed the quiet. I sought out environments where I could bathe in the sound of emptiness.

This haiku is about the new relationship I find myself in since chemo. I am entangled in a tense tango with tinnitus! I had always thought of tinnitus, I now realise unfairly, as a made-up condition. Ringing? In the ears?? Pah!! Let me assure you, it's a real thing. My days of silence are done. The audiologist tells me that platinum-based chemo drugs (for me, Cistplatin) are renowned for it. The hair follicles in my ears are burnt off. They ain't coming back! Couple this with acute hearing loss and, well, you hear what I'm saying (pun intended!).

I find it difficult to express how I feel about this right now. I am doing my best to adjust to the new normal. I waited 50 years to explore the art of silence. I lived believing I was entitled to both the presence of sound and its absence. I felt I had some right to choose when I switch it on and when I switch it off. I see now that I am not entitled to anything. That, my dear friend, is one hell of a life lesson.

**the last ember passed
a bitter chill gripped our home
and we watched you soar**

My dad was a stoic character. He gave little insight into the terrain of his own heart and soul. That path was off-limits to anyone other than himself. Actually, I don't even think he dared venture into his own heart. His incessant striving for ascent meant he would push and push; never to be beaten or overcome by any adversity he faced. This was a mighty inner force he wielded. On many occasions I found myself in awe of him and his capacity for accomplishment. The most time he had off of work in his life was when he had his appendix removed and that was only 1 day. The day after his surgery!

When he received his own renal cancer diagnosis back in 2011, it broke his already fragile heart. Having no method to voice his pain meant that each salty tear was pushed back inside. Salt erodes and his already ruptured body was unable to withstand it.

My heart broke too. I had to watch my dad, who so desperately wanted his kite to soar again, remain flightless. After 9 months of a gruelling fight against descent, my dad left for his final ascent. I sat with him. I stroked his brow. Like polaroid snaps, our times together flashed through. And then he took flight.

How easy it is to forget the fragility of life and the exquisite privilege it is to live it. I wonder, if we truly honoured the bounty that rests in each heart beat we are gifted, how might we choose to live differently?

racing through my veins
wheel spins then handbrake turns
no regard for life

When I was growing up, my mum and dad bought a small flat in the sleepy market town of Wimborne, Dorset. It had belonged to an aunt of my dad who had passed away. The average age of Wimborne's population is 104. It's packed with gift shops, card shops, tea shops and ladies' dress shops. There's a hotel; 2 pubs. The most interesting thing to have ever happened there is that somebody sat at a regulars' table in the tea rooms. It all kicked off. People were throwing napkins and all sorts. Someone even called the police but then discovered that the local bobby had been on holiday since 1952.

But on a Friday night, it would all come to life. Wimborne became Dorset's playground for souped-up compact cars. Booming stereos, go-faster stripes, extravagant paint jobs, monster truck alloys, neon lights, inflated spoilers and the obligatory tinted windows. This slow-paced town morphed into a race track. The young, mostly boys, seized the thrill of racing at top speed around mini roundabouts and one-way systems. Like peacocks, they would preen and parade themselves. Displays of arrogant willy-waving filled the once-quiet streets.

Full of swagger, they carry a total disregard for life as they barge their way through. The faster they can fly and the more they can take out, the better. They don't care. They have a solo mission: to prove they are better than anyone else.

The long list of chemo drugs I was given bulldozed into my bloodstream. Knocking out everything in their path. Their souped-up engines primed to go faster.

I was never *boy* enough to be a boy racer. Although my Vauxhall Nova 1.0 did have an orange stripe down the side. Actually, I despised the boys as I could never equal their macho aggression and flouncing *look at me* vibe.

In the same way, on so many occasions, I hated chemotherapy. I despised the way it barbarically hammered my body.

---

the sun bows its head
as we enter the dark night
new dawns always rise

Yule begins on the winter solstice on Wednesday 21st December, and with that marks the longest night of the year and the welcoming back of the sun. In Norse traditions, Yule is the time of the rebirth of the sun.

The winter solstice's longest night calls us into a state of reflection, marking a new year as the season begins to shift. For me, it offered a moment to find my rhythm again. 2022, with chemo cycles, scans galore, an SCT and then maintenance treatment, felt like all rhythm had been lost. The year had been crammed with chaos and a sense of not quite knowing what is next. We would have a plan and then it all changed. And then changed again. One moment I felt better, then terrible. A routine PICC line clean turned into being admitted for 4 days because of dangerously low platelets. And so it went on …

The solstice gifts us a chance to pause. To slow down, even if for only a few minutes. It offers the possibility of a soft reset. I remember singing choral pieces as a teenager. Sometimes I would lose my harmony line and rhythm. I could fight with it to get back in. Or I could mime for a few bars, tread water until I could find the rhythm and musical line once more. The solstice offers us this too.

I wrote this haiku especially for a winter solstice ceremony that Kelly and I attended. I shared it with the group, screwed it up into a ball and offered it to the flames. On reflection, the haiku acts as a reminder to us of how hope is always present, despite not always being able to clutch it tight. The days always end and, before too long, the sun will rise again. Nature knows exactly what to do. It teaches us well.

I wonder where you might need to find your rhythm again? Where are you fighting? In what ways are you singing *out of time?* Take a beat. Catch your breathe. Listen. Listen for the whispers.

SPRING

oubaitori: the Japanese concept that people, like flowers, bloom in their own time and in their own individual ways

After the cold and dark of winter months, signs of new life begin to emerge; bare, frost-covered branches begin to develop new buds and shoots; ash, beech and oak buds start to burst; the delicate blossoms of crab apple and blackthorn awaken; we see the cuckoo flower and bluebells set about their mission to bloom, adding to the riot of seasonal colour; crocuses spring up from the depths of the moist soil; the first of the queen bumblebees emerge from their hibernation; all manner of seasonal creepy crawlies come out to play, including beetles, spiders and ladybirds; newly born lambs bounce through the fields, wobbling on unsteady legs and calling to their mothers for support and reassurance; squirrels leap from tree to tree; migratory birds return to the UK after a winter spent in warmer climes—look out for sand martins and chiff-chaffs; blackbirds and blue-tits start to architect and build their new homes; the weary hum of the mowers as they chug into action for the first cut of the year. You don't need to look far to be reassured and hopeful that brighter days are on the horizon.

For us inhabitants of Planet Earth, it is now our moment to be yawning, stretching and waking ourselves from a time of hibernation. If flowers can begin to push their way through, then surely this is a time for us to flourish too. The days where we no longer need 4 thermal layers, a hat and scarf are a blessing. As rhubarb pushes through, we fill our bellies with sugary spring delights. Darker days are fewer and we are guided towards more light. Vitamin D starts to soak in through our skin and caress our bodies, soothing the dryness that has come from months of artificial heat. The increased light suppresses melatonin production and we start to feel more alert and energised. This phase is one of clearing out and decluttering: our homes, our minds, our bodies and our hearts.

We bustle and bristle with a little more lightness. There is perhaps, as the season suggests, a little more spring in our step.

My own signs of new growth are sparse. I remain naked.

you dare to mesmerise
your silky deliciousness
cake i adore thee

H ere I was, breaking my haiku virginity. I was just 4 days old following my stem cell transplant! It was May 14th, 2022. I had been isolated in a hospital room for 10 days solid and was going ever so slightly mad, sat on the bed, gently rocking and wondering when and if this would all be over. My mood swings felt intense. Locked in a cell, I felt as if my emotions bounced around within an echo chamber. My heart was yelling, but no one heard me.

From a young age, I have been an overthinker. I've worried. I've ruminated until I couldn't ruminate anymore. The exhaustion of it all would then leave me empty. Seconds later, my mind would be filling once more with ideas, plans, stories and action. If you were to buy a ticket into my mind, you'd be asking for a refund. It's an undesirable place. As a child, when I discovered theatre and acting it was the only place in my life where I settled and focused. Nothing could distract my laser-like precision which performance demands. This lasted for many years, right until my ego took a tighter grip and I started to become obsessed with every action and thought. Theatre was no longer a safe haven.

For me and haiku, it was love at first sight. Finally, here was a way in which I could slice through the jumbled noise in my head and gently coax my voice out into the open.

Overthinking, with no visible exit, is costly. It is a thief of joy.

This haiku is a bit silly and was a rare moment of playfulness. It makes me smile whenever I read it, almost as if I reconnected with the wisdom of my inner child as the 17 syllables flowed. Oh, and I do indeed adore cake! Chocolate ideally. Or coffee and walnut. Mostly chocolate.

---◆---

**you stand before me
and i see you in the distance
i hold both dearly**

---◆---

2022 has brought many people into my life whom I would probably never have met if it weren't for my cancer: oncologists, oncology nurses, transplant nurses, radiologists, hospice teams, those walking a similar path, their carers, those who are grieving for loves lost and those who have a desire to show support and love.

You may be an internet scroller who stops to watch the new puppy video. Cooing, awwwwws and a certain level of gushing takes place. Then you move on. Perhaps feeling a little richer for the experience and touched in some way by the beauty of new life. There are those who will just scroll on by, not bothered by puppies. Unchanged.

I was the new puppy. Some stopped to gawp. Some to be moved. Some folks' lives will have been transformed by my story. And do you know what, only a few people could see me beyond my illness, beyond the hair loss, beyond my tears. They could see me in my nearness but could also envision who I was becoming. Peeling away layers that revealed new life. Like bifocal glasses; the gift of seeing both near and far.

The eminent psychiatrist Roberto Assagioli spoke of the importance in seeing the client with *bifocal vision*: widening our lens so that we can see both the personality that is present and the soul that is wanting to emerge. It is easy to spot the neuroses, the problems and the wounds. But with these also sit the treasures, the talents and the essential qualities. Viewing the world bifocally perhaps affords us all the opportunity to look and notice with far greater understanding.

If we were all to take some responsibility to live this way, I often wonder to myself how much kinder our world might be …

life can feel knotty
when you abandon your truth
burying it deep

In the few years prior to being diagnosed, I found myself in a state of restlessness. I have often described it as soul tapping me on my shoulder, begging me to wake up. It was a light tap to begin with; losing pieces of work, not getting some I'd expected, a few aches, pains and ills. Over time these increased in both intensity and frequency. It was as if each one was carefully crafted to get my attention. Soul knew I had strayed off path and was becoming increasingly desperate to help me reorient. In truth, I had become estranged from myself. What started out as light taps ended with the grabbing of my balls in a vice. I had no choice but to listen.

Life was, indeed, feeling knotty. I think about my clients from both a corporate arena and from my private practice, and many were also living through various stages of knottiness. A soaring torment from soul that was orchestrated to seize attention. As they battled for more *ups,* they were met with descent. Most people react by turning away and getting more angry with the world they inhabit. Some bravely choose to turn and face themselves.

We will all be summoned to an appointment with soul at some stage in our life. Our narcissistic approach is to brush it off as not important. Soul is relentless in its determination for us to journey home. It continues to send us *missed appointment* reminders, until we choose to show up.

Soul speaks. Soul is always wanting to come through us. Taken hostage by the personality that we have each honed over the years, our true nature patiently waits. As it speaks, it needs us to listen. Eventually, reluctantly, I did. Do you? I mean, do you really listen to the gentle nudges, the light taps and the slightly firmer digs?

---◆---

**don't let your voice be
chased from your wide open throat
let them hear your roar**

---◆---

As a professional speaker, I felt pretty well equipped to roar. I wasn't the type of speaker who made his career via the art of motivational roaring, but if it was a lion that the client needed, I could magic it up.

In the weeks following my diagnosis, my roar was inaudible. I sobbed. Rather like I did when I failed my 11+ but this time, I sobbed inside. From the bottom of my cavern, the small child within me sat cross-legged on the floor and cried. And shouted. And roared. But the sound somehow never made its way up and through my throat. It was stuck. I had been chased back inside by my cancer.

How often it is that we can be chased back inside by something or someone. The overbearing feelings of torment and fear can lead to our lion becoming trapped within. Our own spirit becomes caged. It took many months for my lion to unleash a timid meow. I spent hour upon hour patiently sitting down next to the lion; tenderly offering it presence, believing that at some point it would be ready to open its throat and roar again.

soul softly whispers
as it beckons me closer
let go i've got you

I come to my life with a story that safely and tenderly guides me. Well, I probably didn't arrive with it but stumbled over it along the way. I imagine it belongs to someone else and I pinched it. It goes like this. We are a soul, in a body, having a human experience. Soul choreographs the twists, turns and groovy moves of our life. When our body dies, soul passes over and will, at some point, occupy a new body (human, insect, flower, tree …) and move on to live new experiences. There, that's it. Who needs big books to explain how life works. As I said, it's just my story. Not THE story.

With cancer, comes fear. Mighty amounts of the stuff too. The most commonly pedalled narrative is about *fighting it*; entering into battle with the hostile enemy. It's odd really, at a time where we are at our weakest, there is an air of expectation that we get up and go to war. For most, that is not an option. But hey, don't confuse resisting war with giving up. No, far from it. We did everything within our gift for me to recover and stay in remission. We continue to do so. I have tried to build a different relationship with cancer—one that is about being *with* cancer, as opposed to *fighting* cancer. It relies more on me letting go and trusting soul to have choreographed whatever dance it thinks I need to be involved in.

This haiku is about that. I wrote it at the time when the realisation struck me that I needed to place great faith and trust in my soul. I needed to believe that it was always wanting the best for me, even in times of dark descent. This faith encouraged me to loosen my tight grip on life and what I thought it owed me.

I don't believe that war *catches* people when they need it most—we rely on a brave soldier to step in at the right time. Soul, I believe, will always catch me.

**the light streams through you
your naked beauty revealed
everything exposed**

I have always felt as if forests call me. Yes, you heard right. They personally shout my name and invite me in for a solo exhibition of their sheer magnificence. Where I grew up, we lived next to a newly planted arboretum. Mostly, I thought it was a cool word that I couldn't spell. Until I visited with my dad one day. I was fascinated by the saplings, venturing out into their new life. I'd compare them to the woods on the way up to the brow of Coombe Hill; ancient, wise and with hundreds of years' worth of stories to tell. I would practice drawing trees in hope that I might be able to bring to life some of their magic via my sketchbook.

Without wanting to mark myself as a tree hugger, I do actually enjoy nothing more than sitting down with my back against the trunk, feeling its sturdiness and strength holding me up. I relish the confidence that their firm rootedness will keep me safe.

It is without surprise that during my recuperation, I had urges to visit woodland. On one particular visit, I wandered through and a moment that I would never be able to capture again stole my attention. Rich orange rays of sunlight bounced through the trees like a pinball. Ricocheting from trunk to branch until it eventually fed in through my eyes, reaching down to wrap around my heart. I stood in wonder. The light had Harry Potter powers; magically illuminating all that it caressed.

In times of our own darkness, light has the power to reveal our vulnerabilities. Cancer had brought me into relationship with my own descent. The light and love that I felt from those around me showed me my own vulnerabilities and sensitivities to this human existence. The deep wintering I went through stripped me of every leaf and shelter I had hidden behind. By allowing the light to bounce inside I was able to give a nod to the fragility of life. The fragility of *my* life. And the fragility and wonder that rest within the forest.

One day, I will live in a forest. I know it.

to the heart that aches
the ribcage holds you firm
the mind will be kind

My first *proper* girlfriend was Justine. I was 17. I liked her. I liked her a lot. I bought her a rose for each month we were together. Fortunately, at month 9, after she met a boy on her family holiday to Spain, she dumped me. Actually her mum dumped me. On their front door step. Anyway, the roses were costing me a fortune and I was about to head off into the shiny lights of drama school so, all in all, probably a good thing.

But it was the first time my heart hurt from a loss of love. It was deeply ruptured and wounded and my first experience of heartache. It's a real thing. Who knew. After Justine, I became a master of ignoring my heartaches. There were, frankly, too many.

Cancer. Descent. Facing my own demise. It's as if I was being called to account for all the heartache I'd swerved in the past. The grooves were cut deep, I had no choice but to soothe them.

One of the qualities that has become much stronger and evident in my life this year is that of trust. Trusting others, yes. But mostly, learning to trust myself. My *Self*. My soul. My essence. My body has been brutalised, but my soul remains unharmed. It is, I believe, untouchable. My heart has ached. It still does. But my ribcage, despite everything it has lived through, holds strong. Like an older brother who looks out for his younger sister, it offers constant protection. And my mind, whilst it has drifted (bolted!), is gravitating towards a place of stillness and non-attachment. Like a mill pond. It is full. And quiet. And centred.

Batman and Robin, Fred and Ginger, Morecambe and Wise. Partnerships that can weather the storm. I can add to this list; Mind and Ribcage. Acting as lighthouses, steering the dangers safely around my fragile heart.

here begins the trip
here starts our adventure
cup my hand tightly

*S*hoshin: a concept from Zen Buddhism meaning the beginner's mind. It speaks to the notion of adopting an attitude full of openness, eagerness, curiosity and a lack of preconceptions. It is a paradox. So often, the more we know, the more we can close our own mind to further learning. Zen monk Shunryu Suzuki said, 'In the beginner's mind there are many possibilities, but in the expert's there are few.'

This descent has presented me with numerous beginnings. And glimpses into the end, too. But this haiku is about starting out. My diagnosis day, my first chemo, a lumbar puncture, hair loss, a stem cell transplant, remission. There is an endless list of *firsts*. Each, in its own way, felt consuming. There was no map. No compass. I had been dropped into a barren landscape and expected to find my way out. I was facing not only an unknown outer terrain, but being called to adventure into an intimate inner terrain too. In the past, I'd abandoned myself when the going got tough. This time, it was not an option.

The cupping of a hand that I describe in the haiku is both literal and metaphorical. It brought me great comfort and soothed a wounded part of me that was terrified. This was not only my new beginning, but Kelly and Mia's also.

Each day, the three of us, tightly bound together, would tentatively step out into the new 24-hour cycle that awaited us. The pilgrimage that we had been summoned to make. Our quest was for meaning. It was to find purpose. Some days it was purely one of survival. A central theme of any pilgrimage is internal resilience. It was necessary for each of us to find shelter, hardiness and companionship. This adventure brought enormous vulnerability.

Cupping each other's hands is akin to cupping each other's hearts. Both are an act of love.

Whatever pilgrimage you may be called to make, be it ascent or descent, find the hands that will hold your hands. Find the shoulders that will stand firmly next to yours. Discover the hearts that will hold your own heart; tenderly and kindly.

hope acts as the guide
controlling my progression
from here to my end

Very often, I have a sense of *lostness*. Since being ill, I frequently feel as if life is futile. It feels empty. Desolate. Rudderless, unable to place myself in the world and with no sense of direction to get me some place new.

It is only this year where I feel like I have come into better relationship with hope. I have bandied the word around with little appreciation for what it means to me and my life. How have I built this relationship? By going within. By writing. And more writing. And reading about the experiences of others. And reflecting. And speaking with my therapist. And journeying deeper. And then writing some more. Did I get it from self-help books? No. Perhaps hope was looking to find me as much as I was seeking it.

I have tended to be a little sceptical of hope. I have felt it to be a bit *Pollyanna-esque*! Let's look on the brighter side of total shit!! Hope can easily be more about how we want the world to be—*my life would be perfect if only I could …* Getting lost in this craving can end up separating us from the world even more. Often, when we feel torn apart and shredded, remaining hopeful feels like a useless place to put our energy. The number of people who have rattled off the notion of 'well, you gotta stay hopeful!' Have I? Really?!

I am learning to see my world with equanimity. Equanimity means balance, and it's the balance that is born of wisdom. It reminds us that what is happening in front of us is not the end of the story. It is just all that we can see right now. This moment will pass.

Hope is not a solo expedition. Hope lives strong when we come into communion with others. It is found deep in the heart of tribes.

I am practising holding hope lightly. It is helping me locate North on the compass. I've had bleak times of descent before and, in one way or another, they resolved themselves. I know that I have the quality of resilience within me. We all do. It's not a superpower that only I have. But sometimes it likes to play hide-and-seek with us because with resilience comes vulnerability. And that, for so many of us, is unbearable.

**my tired body
restless from the gaps of this
incomplete story**

Each day, I question how long *this* will last. *This cancer. My cancer.* I wake up, hoping that maybe it only existed in my vivid dreams. But it's very real. And even though some days I now feel fairly well and certainly have regained a little of the *Quiff Richard* look (which means everyone acts as if nothing ever happened), each day has sequences that feel laboured, painful and like I'm all at sea.

In recent weeks I have described to my therapist a strange sensation that I frequently have. I can, mid activity/conversation, hear another part of myself saying 'what's the point, forget it, it's all fruitless anyway.' I'm staying patient with what this might be and the meaning it contains. Who is it within me? What are they wanting me to pay attention to? What purpose does it serve? The experience can last mere seconds but the residue hangs around. It is as if I am injected with anxiety that then hurtles through my veins. It certainly grabs my attention and amplifies my worries with being in remission; what's next, for how long, how will I navigate the spaces?

Learning to tolerate my incomplete story is a daily lesson in patience for me. The paradox that comes with incompleteness; discomfort and growth potential can be tough to digest.

This story of mine is full of gaps. As I look back over 50 years and forward towards another … who knows how many I will be fortunate enough to have. There are intervals and interludes, cavities and holes. Imagine getting totally absorbed by the most gripping novel, only to find that pages are missing. Even some chapters. I guess you could fill in the blanks yourself but there remains a sense of being short-changed. A state of wondering what you have missed out on.

Where are the gaps in your own story? What creative endeavours might support you to understand these gaps? If you were authoring your own future story, what would you include?

**resting with the trees
listening to their wisdom
breezes stir my soul**

Regardless of whether I had icicles hanging from my nose or puddles of sweat running down between my thighs, I was the child to be found in a T-shirt and shorts. Come rain, wind or tropical British summertime, I lived in skimpy clothing. As I've grown older, I have come to relish warmer climes. I feel the pull of balmy summer days, a deep tan and the way that the heat just makes my whole soul tingle. Bliss. Winters have never troubled me. I'll happily stick on a hat and some gloves if I sense a shivery expedition ahead.

And then I had chemotherapy and a stem cell transplant. And it was here that my weather-proofing was lost. This past winter was brutal. Each day and night was spent being cold to the core. My bones hurt. I have never invested in so many warmth-giving items; blankets, hand warmers, thicker-than-thick socks made for Inuits, insulated pants, long johns, nose warmers, willy warmers, and electric feet warmers made for the over 70s. Winter hurt.

And look, here comes summer. Fans, ice, cool tops, shaders and total nakedness. Summer sun hurts too. Jeez.

Just down the road from where we live, I have discovered a tiny patch of woodland. I am the only person who knows it is there (I like to believe) and when I enter this minute kingdom, I somehow settle back into my body. The trees greet me. 'Hello old friend,' they say with some jollity. Their branches hugging me tight. They offer solitude. They assure me that whatever I am carrying today, I can leave with them. They can bear it. The air is cool and fragrant. I breathe and my lungs fill with oxygen, my cells bristle with delight. I'm present and I feel extremely human. It's all just as it should be; not hot, not cold. The trees revel in my openness to their stories. Some of the younger ones rolling their tree hollows with the exhaustion that comes from having heard these tales, countless times.

Amongst these friends of mine, I stumble into small clearings. Spaces between the notes. Places of rest. A quietening. This vital gap between what was and what is ahead.

I leave replenished. What was probably just 10 minutes feels like countless hours of equilibrium. Despite the spring breeze, I hardly even notice the chill in my body. I am merely content with the aliveness that I feel.

it looks like a door
i stand in trepidation
frightened by the loss

I've always been fascinated by liminality and liminal spaces. Liminal comes from the Latin word 'limen', which means *threshold*. A liminal space is the time between 'what was' and 'what's next'. It is a place of transition, a time of waiting and not knowing the future.

Richard Rohr describes this space as, 'where we are betwixt and between the familiar and the completely unknown. There alone is our old world left behind, while we are not yet sure of the new existence. That's a good space where genuine newness can begin.'

The trouble is, liminal spaces don't generally feel good. And this one is no different. I have described a few times during this year my sense of walking a corridor. There are multiple doors. At least they look like doors. Zero signage and seemingly no easy way to peek inside.

Often, I loiter for a while. I have a concern that they might not even lead into a room. Perhaps they are a sharp drop into a void. Or maybe they lead to yet another corridor. Another liminal space that takes me to who knows where. This space that is *betwixt and between* fills me with anxious thoughts and extra heartbeats. Like a death row prisoner, kitted out in their orange romper suit, shuffling along towards their last supper. Approaching the unknown.

I did choose to walk through the doors. No steep drops. No Stars In Your Eyes rock star feel either. Just images. Voices. Some movies running. Rooms that revealed my imminent death. Others that showed me a future full of rapture and aliveness.

I like it. Despite the trepidation that each door holds, I am becoming comfortable with the idea that I can leave the room, as well as enter it. Each one offers me a glimpse into potential future scenarios.

Walking a liminal path is unlikely to ever be a breeze. We will always be tested as to how we sit with ambiguity and the *pick n mix* nature of life. One moment a Strawberry Lace, the next a Liquorice Allsort.

**tiny droplets move
meeting their mighty future
in something bigger**

I used to live close to the River Mole in Surrey. It is a tributary of the River Thames. It's not too shabby at almost 80 km long. It was first recorded in AD 983. It has a long history, that's for sure. Our garden backed onto it and most days during the summer I would jump in our canoe to paddle a little way upstream. Five minutes along and I would float around in Surrey paradise. A small haven of biodiversity. It felt compact. A gentle rhythm to the water. If I didn't actively paddle, I would simply levitate alongside the water boatmen.

If I paddled in the other direction, there was a robustness to the current. It had a pull like I was being sucked into the vortex of the Thames. Little me was being seduced to enter something larger and far mightier.

We begin life as a small stream. Shallow. Giggling drops of water converge to become a small river. We meander through life, following the twists and turns that the riverbed and its banks provide us with. This can continue for a lifetime and can bring years of playful joy.

For most of us, sooner or later, we are called to join the Herculean river of our life. A moment where we are brought into relationship with a depth, grandeur and force that are only seen in our larger waterways. Who knows in what form our calling will appear? They are often in disguise and can, to begin with, be ignored. Eventually, the roar and the force becomes all-consuming and there is little we can do but follow the tributary.

Cancer has been resolute in bringing me to my knees. I mean this in respect of both the turmoil it brought and the reverence I found. I have a deeper respect for life. All life, not just mine.

And so, I paddle on. The great river of life will, I am confident, afford me the opportunities for stillness and calm on the surface, underpinned by the depth and strength of who I am becoming.

SUMMER

wabi-sabi: this central concept in Japanese aesthetics comes from Buddhist teachings on the transient nature of life; a pot with uneven edges is more beautiful than a perfectly smooth one, because it reminds us that life is not perfect

SUMMER

Our natural world buzzes, shimmies and toots its horn to salute the entrance of balmy summer days; the crowns of the trees reach over us, offering welcome shelter from the intensity of the heat; spring flowers step aside to make way for the rainbow of summer blooms; honeysuckle bursts into life, its sweet-smelling fragrance seducing the bees, butterflies and moths to get merry on its nectar; baby birds tentatively take their first flaps into adulthood; the heavenly sweetness hiding in flowers is a haven for delicate and lustrous butterflies; bats swoop through the night-time on their hunt for insects to feed their young; summer isn't summer without the chirp chirp of the grasshopper; grass snakes twist and turn amongst the undergrowth; the soft soothing hum of bumblebees; daisy chains and rock pooling. Summer is a sensory feast.

The middle of the year. The season that reveals nature at its most full. A time for us to enjoy being at full bloom. We can collect the bountiful crops from our gardens and from our soul. All the energy and effort from our planting starts to come to fruition. We can literally reap what we have sown. School holidays allow families to both restore and revitalise, making the most of quality time together. New adventures, street parties and BBQs offer the opportunity to connect with new friends and community. Holidays afford us the space to author and craft the second half of the year; what are my hopes, dreams and wishes for the next 6 months? The increased range of fruits in the markets and shops, salads and summer veg, encourages us to fill our bodies with goodness. Drinking extra water supports us to flood out toxins and increase our vitality.

With glowing skin and a refreshed body, we are ready to tackle the remainder of the year.

My glow remains absent. An already desolate landscape has been stripped of the growth that tries to push through. With chemo and a transplant close up in my rear-view mirror, there is little evidence of seasonal bloom.

**sweet strawberry moon
heralding in summertime
illuminating**

It goes by many names: strawberry moon, honey moon, flower moon, planting moon. The June moon has always felt like it garnered respect. It helps mark out an important threshold between the ending of spring and the opening of summer. Strawberry moon refers to the ripening of the berries that bound into life in June. This month also sees the summer solstice. Considered to be a fertile time for all on Planet Earth. In Eastern traditions they refer to it as the lotus moon—it is seen to represent purity, beauty and enlightenment.

Since I was a child, I have held a deep fascination about the moon and the stars. I'd often spend hours gazing out of my window, watching the full moon captivate us with its beauty. It was totally enchanting. I was drenched in its spell. I longed for a telescope. But given the choice by my parents, I opted for new tap shoes. Oh, the life of a performer …

From a celestial perspective, June is a busy month. It also happened to be the first month I was home following my own *re-birth day*. Like many nights around this time, I was Sleepless in Surrey, often lying awake, dreaming of better days and holding more genuine hope about my recovery than I'd had for a while. The brightness of the moon on this night drew me in. From where I lay, it had tucked itself up into the corner of our bedroom window. Kelly slept soundly beside me, resting deeply and making the most of a quiet night with zero snoring! My moon: I call it mine as on this particular night I believed it was here purely to help illuminate my path. Its sole purpose was to show me the way. It offered reassurance that following so much death and decay in my body, new growth was beginning to appear. I bathed in its glory and greatness. Each cell danced a happy dance with feelings of being replenished.

Whilst there is not always a full moon to bathe in, there are many other ways we can be recharged: people, nature, sunlight, good food, water, kindness. Most of all, love. Always love. If you need to be replenished, I encourage you to seek out whatever you need to restore your body, mind and soul.

Strawberry Moon 2022, thank you.

with eyes on the prize
path shining in the sunlight
a gift of silver

There is a handful of happenings every year in June that symbolises the start of summer: swifts; Pimms with mint; tiny flower buds on the tomato plants; pink and white dog roses filling the hedge; the first radishes; elderflowers peeking through. But early summer days would not be the same without snails. Hundreds of them. Zigzagging across our garden in their endeavours to create a silver map of every London Underground station in existence.

Without fail, my first footstep of the day out into our garden and, there they are. The remaining night-shift workers on their way home. Behind them, a glistening and resplendent trail imprinted on our patio, paths and grass. Hours of work has gone into this tapestry.

I always imagine that they must have worked so very hard and relentlessly to have crafted this for us. And soon, with our clumsy human footsteps, the dog and his roly-polys and the warmth of the summer sun, they are erased. Following a few hours of snail snoozing, they will soon be back on it.

They never appear to work hard and fast. It seems as if they work hard and slow. They are meticulous. They are graceful. There is no rushing. No haste. Just a regal presence and gliding. It feels a far cry from my once familiar life of frantic overloading.

I watch them and I wonder what it is they are teaching me. Perhaps it is for me to ensure I leave my own majestic trail whilst

I am here. Maybe it is a reminder that whenever I think I am not leaving a trail, I am; majestic or otherwise. Or do they want me to move more slowly? Slower than that. Slower still. Or is it that they want me to stay detached from all that I do, knowing it will soon be erased and replaced by a newer version anyway? And that's ok. Or do they hope that I continue to weave my own sublime and joyful life tapestry, in whatever way I am pulled to do? Maybe it is all of these and none of these.

we simply don't know
by taking the scenic route
what beauty we see

I like to dawdle. Potter. Mooch. Whatever you want to name it. I've always enjoyed it. No agenda, no outcomes, no goals to hit. Just some space to, well, dawdle. Part of the beauty of dawdling is that we don't quite know where we will arrive. Or what exactly we might see on our travels. The trouble is, I didn't give myself permission to dawdle.

Dawdling can be defined as idle. Loitering. Slow. And in a world that celebrates fast and then even faster, slow has no place.

Part of the issue with our 'up up up' culture, is that we become gripped by a destination. Almost fixated on a dot in the distance. Our entire field of vision narrows to this one small point. Everything either side, above and below, becomes blurred out, as if they are body parts we should not be feasting our eyes upon. The trouble with this is that we are never quite sure what we are excluding. What are we not seeing? And if we are not seeing it, what are we missing out on? Our hearts can lose their hunger to be creative. The scenic route or, as I prefer to call it, The Dawdlers Way, offers us a path of beauty, allowing our imaginations to be fuelled and our hearts to be filled.

Prior to being ill, I was a number in the race. I surged from idea to outcome to goal. I believed my value was in the pace I moved, my accumulation of tasks ticked off and the accolades received. The more I did, the more I would be loved and admired. Surely. That's a universal truth, right?

Having this year dominated by a snail's pace has shown me what total nonsense this is and revealed how some aspects of my childhood and the trauma it contained taught me that rather out-of-date story. I have now entered life once more, happier to walk The Dawdlers Way ...

I am convinced that the art of dawdling has been lost and needs reinvigorating. Our planet is demanding that we slow down. How do you include time and space and permission in your life to slow down? Almost ... to ... a ... standstill.

snap i hear you break
the dead pulled from the living
new buds spring to life

What my dad was unable to teach me around the quality of patience, descent and kite-flying, he made up for with his passion and joy of gardening. Sadly, I wasn't interested. Despite regular visits to my uncle's garden centre and his full-bodied enthusiasm for shrubs, I was pulled only towards the whiff of greasepaint and the opportunity to wear coloured leg warmers.

How I wish I'd listened. I find myself at 50 years of age trying to spot the difference between a shrub and a weed. Kelly encourages me to keep everything that grows in our garden whilst I am convinced it is dead and want to dig it up.

Following my SCT, we all had to isolate in Tyler Towers for 3 whole months. Fortunately it was the summer and we could at least enjoy what Mother Earth had gifted us with. As I wandered around the weeds (shrubs) I started to snap the dead rose buds from their stems. I had some distant recollection of my dad explaining the importance of deadheading and how it spurred on new growth. I had no idea if this was correct, but it felt that deadheading was the way to go.

Roll on a couple of months and just as summer wrapped, our rose bush has exploded again. I have never seen so many buds. We have had to build a scaffold structure to hold it upright as it topples under the weight of succulent pink petals.

It reminds me as to the importance of removing what is dead in our lives. Snap off the old to make space for the new.

Behaviours, stories, beliefs, values, relationships, patterns. If they are no longer of service, then find the courage to remove them. Doing so will clear the way for the new to come into existence. All too often we hold on simply because it is familiar and comfortable, both of which are important. And both of which have the power to stifle and suffocate.

---

like Fred and Ginger
you glide with ease and beauty
interlaced as one

The word *suite,* in my mind, implies luxury. The best of the best. A place where beautiful memories are made. Somewhere that oozes opulence and grandeur. A chemo suite, however, is not quite the same. The ones I've hung out in certainly ooze love. Well, mostly. They are otherwise places where tremendously difficult and painful memories are stamped. And, therefore, snippets of joy and lightness stand out.

During one of my Friday visits, I sat opposite a lady who I later came to know was called Debbie. She hadn't long been diagnosed and this Friday was her first visit to the *suite.* She commented on my T-shirt which was adorned with the slogan *It's OK to feel SHIT.* 'I love it … where can I get one?' I agreed to give her the name of the website. We laughed and connected over funny T-shirt slogans. And feeling shit. We didn't need to mention how cancer also connected us.

Now, pottering off to the loo when you are attached to a drip stand can be challenging. Debbie got herself up and ready to head to the loo. What happened next was 30 seconds of beauty and joy. Her stand had become entangled amongst the numerous wires and tubes. In her eagerness to free herself, Debbie entered into a beautiful dance with the drip stand. They moved, twisted, shimmied and caressed. They were Fred & Ginger. I smiled as I watched something, which should have been uncomfortable to witness, evolve into a magnificent sequence of choreography. I shared with Debbie the utter joy I got from their performance.

She smiled. She was touched by how I had noticed this moment of detail in her life.

A week later, I bought her the T-shirt and left it with the chemo nurses to pass on. I never saw her again. I hope she got the T-shirt. I hope her life is a little less shit. I hope she is still entwined in a beautiful dance with life. But I just don't know. Thank you Debbie.

haiku are simple
and sometimes they don't make sense
peas and plum on toast

Silliness can hold the power to break tension. Pointless laughter and schoolboy sniggering have helped get me through the shittiest hours. The day I wrote this haiku was heavy for me. It was one of my tough moments during chemo where I wasn't sure how much more I could take. I looked around for the Exit sign. The haiku that poured out of me were generally dark. I was then brought in a dish of hospital dinner that was beyond description. It was horrendous. I've actually no idea what the plate contained. They weren't food types I was familiar with. Once, in a Hong Kong food market, I had a plate of something that looked like eyeballs and brain. I could be forgiven for not knowing as I couldn't read or speak the language. Here, in Tooting, I could both read and speak. But it still wasn't clear how the food matched the description on the menu. And here I was: sob uncontrollably or piss my pants with laughter. Peas and plum would have tasted better together than the mess I'd been offered.

Life can be both utterly joyful and gut-twistingly painful. Often at the same time. My own leaning towards deep self-reflection frequently renders me lost in tears and melancholy. I know this. I've known this for 50 years. I therefore know I need to work harder to acknowledge the lightness that is all around me.

Living through dark times can be so corrosive to our hearts. Like the M25, arteries get blocked with the constant stream of traffic. Frantic drivers, desperate to get somewhere, end up getting nowhere. Movement grinds to a halt. This motorway was not built as a car park. The same is perhaps true with our hearts. They are meant to move and pump vital life force to where it is needed most. Humour, play and laughter can be the antidote to feeling blocked and stuck.

how i needed you
so hidden away from sight
one last Haribo

For months I lived in tracksuit bottoms. Joggers. Loose-fitting day wear. If it wasn't joggers, it probably meant it was a bed day for me so I'd sport pyjamas instead. Jeans were a thing of the past. Some days, it was as much as I could do to slip on joggers and get myself off to hospital. Who knew that the struggle for me to lift one leg would be a real thing.

Eventually, jeans made a return to my life. The first pair I grabbed appeared to be unwashed and had probably been slung away around the time of my diagnosis. I slipped them on. My attention seized by how my already twig-like legs now had a vein-like appearance. When your belt wraps around your waist 17 times, it's a sure sign you've lost weight. And then the moment of magic that caught me by surprise.

Deep within my front pocket, I found it. My fingers drawn to the stickiness of something that probably shouldn't have been there. Was it alive? Perhaps an insect who had always fancied sporting a pair of Levis. An old chewing gum? Nope. No, something so much more delightful. One. Last. Haribo. The runt of the Haribo litter. The *unchosen* one. But here it was, waiting for me. The loyal soldier who waited to be told that the war had ended. And it was mine, all mine. Having surgically detached it from the denim and picked away the fluff, I could savour the complete delight of this sweet. I'm a fan of a strong chew and this old Haribo delivered.

The bliss and elation that can come in such unexpected ways has helped carry me through this period of descent. Hidden notes, chance meetings, surprise gifts, enchanted encounters and even a lost Haribo. Life holds such wonder. Much of the time, we are so consumed with playing the notes that we stop noticing the magic that patiently occupies the spaces in between. Hoping to be found.

in golden rapture
teasing me with summer air
hello dragonfly

I'm writing a book about descent. It is a tale of a tragically dark passageway of time in my life. It's about facing the very stark reality of my own death. Sooner than I'd planned for! It's about suffering. It talks to the very harrowing aspect of being human and how nothing lasts forever. It reveals, to you, my season of wintering.

Perhaps this is why I found writing haiku about my summering excruciating. Rather like the mildly obsessive people who scour beaches for gold with metal detectors, I've scrambled around for splinters of light. Some I will have overlooked as I deemed them to be too insignificant, others glimmered and shimmered in resplendent beauty and I couldn't help but linger on them.

On a Sunday morning in late June, our garden filled with the hum of a dragonfly. I could hear it before I could see it. But then my eyes settled on the pure awesomeness of a golden dragonfly. With its delicate lacy wings, it put on a display, just for me. The brilliance of its metallic body was worth more to me than any precious metal. My heavy heart lightened. And then, as fast as it had arrived, it took flight. Graceful and agile, off it danced.

My heart was touched. For the entire morning, the dragonfly played hide-and-seek. I followed it, wanting to soak up every ounce of the wonder it gifted me.

We can easily look for the big, the bold and the glamorous ways of bringing light and joy into our lives. But when we move beyond looking and start to truly *see,* we begin to notice how the world around us is full of gems. And despite the darkness and the descent we may be living through, we can take comfort that the magic and the lightness are longing to be seen.

Hello summertime …

play bigger i said
no no not that big i said
i'm sorry i said

My in-patient chemo cycles would, without exception, hit me hard. I'd already lost any signs of having once been a human with hair. My body wilted under the weight of toxicity. And to top it off, I had to forgo one of the yearly opportunities to hear Mia sing at school. Singing and theatre was one of the ways that Mia and I connected, so to have that plug pulled hurt me. Kelly filmed it, Mia sang and I could do nothing but gush out the sadness of having to miss this concert.

I arrived home 3 days later feeling a little sorry for myself. Mia rocked up from school, chucked down her bags and ventured up to me, in bed, to tell me all about it. We watched the video and talked about her performance and most of the other performances from that night. 'You're amazing,' I said, 'your voice gets stronger and stronger. Incredible.'

'I know I am!' she retorted. And it was at this juncture, without a pause or a thought and a haughty tone, that I said it. 'Don't be a smarty pants Mia, nobody likes a smarty pants!' In the following few seconds, I watched Mia close down and shrivel.

Fuck it. I knew exactly what I'd just done. Worse, I knew that I had done this to her many times before. Why did I see it? How did I see it?! Because I had spoken to myself in the very same way for most of my life. 'Don't be a smarty pants Richard. No one likes a show off.' I'd sent a barrage of push-and-pull messages to little me for as long as I could remember. 'Play Big. Play bigger. No. Not that big. Smaller. Smaller still. Why are you playing so small? Play Big.' And on, and on, and on. It is one thing dishing out this mantra to myself and quite another to be setting Mia up with an identical story.

I marinated in the regret. For her and for me. I asked her to pop up and see me. I told her how sorry I was. She says she didn't even notice. Her mind may not have, her heart would have felt the puncturing.

I have since caught myself on the edge of saying this to Mia again. Just in time, I was able to slam on the brakes. And for me also. Before I crashed head on into more damage, I have stopped myself. Like chemo drugs, these stories are toxic. Their residue remains. We owe it to ourselves to spot them, understand their intention, and endeavour to set them free.

**at the darkest point
in the middle of the night
hold me close my love**

As a child, I don't recall being hugged. We weren't a huggy kind of family. I didn't see my mum hug my dad. I didn't observe them ever strolling hand in hand. There wasn't much human contact. I was, I think, touch starved. With touch playing such a primary role in our human journey, it is no surprise that a lack of it can affect the central nervous system and our psychological, physical and emotional development.

Descent generally brings about feelings of fear, isolation, anxiety, loneliness and instability. If we are to include descent in our lives in ways that allow us to reap its benefits and wisdom, then we must understand how we can best venture through it. One of the ways is through human contact. This might mean the physical touch and closeness of others and it might be about the contact that comes when we feel *seen* and treated as though we matter. Take as an example our 3-year global pandemic that restricted contact in unimaginable ways. It cost each of us. It cost humanity.

My descent through cancer left me feeling isolated. I have already spoken of this feeling of being *unfindable.* I craved contact. Some nights, all Kelly needed to do was to hold my hand or stroke my hair. At other times, I needed her to hold my entire body. Whilst I know that Kelly has my back, always, I needed her to hold my spine firmly with the weight and energy of her body. In most instances, there were no words that could cradle my frightened heart. But the reassurance of her physical presence and love went a long way in comforting me.

Enduring love is rare. I am fortunate to have found it with Kelly. Her touch. Her tenderness. Like Russian dolls, our hearts remain cupped within each other's.

Not everyone is fortunate enough to have a love in their life in quite the way that I do. It is therefore vital that we find ways in which our communities and our systems offer human contact to each other. I am certain that being able to tolerate and bear descent in our lives requires the exchange of a deeply profound love.

we sing our sad song
one beautiful voice holds us
hurting but hopeful

L earning how to make moment by moment choices to connect with the people around us at work, with family, even with the random people you pass on the street, has the potential to be the drops of water that will collectively create an ocean of change in the way we relate to each other, and ultimately to our overall health and wellbeing.

The Roseto effect is a remarkable story of a little Italian town in Roseto, Pennsylvania. Throughout the mid-twentieth century, it was discovered that the inhabitants of Roseto were far healthier than most equivalent communities in the United States. After numerous studies to isolate variables such as diet and genetics, it was concluded that it was ultimately their sense of community that contributed to the residents' overall health. I love this research—the quality and connection of our community literally changes our health outcomes.

The quality and connection of my family (blood and soul) has, without a doubt, been central to getting my body into remission. Fact. We *sang* as one. Healing circles united around the intention of my recovery. Groups of those who love me congregated to discuss ways they could remain steadfast in this passageway of need.

The Roseto effect reveals a compelling glimpse into what can happen when a community acts with one voice and comes together in service of self, other and the wider good. My heart sinks when I look around and see barbaric acts of hatred, war, terror and self-centred action. How have we come to live like this? Which aspect of the Roseto effect would we each need to pull inside, in order that we change what is outside of us?

My family. My friends. My community. Thank you. Thank you for coming together. Whilst our song has been one of despair, it has helped fill me with hope.

**weeds amongst the plants
hard to separate sometimes
like people really**

In our garden, we have 2 beautiful flower beds just outside the back of our house. They are the first thing you see when you step into our suburban oasis. In the summer, they literally bulge with green goodies. Stems standing to attention, ready for inspection, holding up the weight of the lollipop blooms that are poised on top. They wait for their adoring fans to pass and comment on their breathtaking beauty. They squeeze themselves in like this patch is the best patch in town. I love it. It makes my heart sing.

And then look closer. Nestled amongst the lollipops hide the weeds. At first, they are easily missed. They freeze as if they are a bit part in *Squid Game*, terrified that they might be shot. Some of them I can reach. Those that I can, I yank out. Others escape my beady eyes and are safe for another day. Don't get me wrong, the full effect of the green blanket, weeds or otherwise, is spectacular. But sometimes, we just don't want weeds. Often I'm left scratching my head as to which ones are weeds anyway. I hear my dad tutting and puffing. He puts a red cross next to my name and writes 'could do better'.

Beauty is subjective. You might like the weeds. You might not enjoy my lollipop blooms.

I wrote this haiku as I was so struck by the splendour of our garden. And then it got me thinking. Amongst the beauty in our society, are the weeds. The things that need removing. They take shelter behind the beautiful blooms. They live in disguise. Often we are unable to distinguish between weed or wallflower. We may include people in the list of weeds to remove from our life. Or perhaps they are qualities and behaviours: greed, aggression, dishonesty, violence. You can add to the list.

But take heed, every life form has a role. They have a purpose or they wouldn't be here. We need to spot the weeds and the flowers. This requires us to look closer. And before we just pluck anything out, check its role. It almost certainly has one.

entwine your bodies
dance like nothing else matters
hold each other firm

Without a shadow of a doubt, I remain here, alive, because of Kelly. It is with her tenacity, her persistence, her constant striving for solutions to problems and her cavernous love, that I live to see another day.

When I first set eyes and heart on Kelly, I knew what we were destined for. Kelly and I joke about 'you know when you know'. And sometimes, that is just how it is. There is no explanation. There is no justification for a love that feels like it has always existed, long before we knew each other on this physical plane. We have, somehow, always been connected. I was confident that should anything happen in our life that needed us to pull even closer towards each other, we would. Without conditions, we just would. I would have preferred us to not have needed to put that notion to the test, but I guess the universe needed us to know.

There is an *isness* to our relationship. It just is. We just are. And it is with that conviction and our shared partnership, that we dance as one. I would say sing, but Kelly says she can't sing. Although I can't dance. Anyway, between us, we sing and dance through our story. Do we trip over each other's clumsy feet? Do we sing bum notes? Yes and yes! That's ok. We remain as one.

Kelly doesn't appreciate the limelight. She would say she lurks behind the scenes, ensuring everything is in order so that the magic can happen onstage.

Kelly, I don't have the words to convey to you the quality of the love I hold in my heart for you. There are no words. In each cell of my being, I give my life to you in the same ways you have given your life to me. Every day, you teach me what it means to hold another soul, front and centre. My hope is that we have lived through the darkest turmoil any partnership needs to test its resolve. We survived. We passed. Thank the lord I found you. You are perfectly and precisely all that I waited for.

The pieces of the puzzle that you lack are waiting inside of you, ready for someone to find them again. Hold firm. At times you may feel jumbled, but everything you need is there. Ready. Poised.

knowledge is power
yet this belief keeps us stuck
play is what we lack

When I look back at my childhood, I see a boy who took life fairly seriously. I was a sensitive lad and if others looked like they were struggling, I'd look to help. 'Great quality to have' I hear you say. 'That is the spirit of a fine young man!' Yes, I think it is. Well, it's certainly one end of the see-saw. But when it is so painfully out of kilter with the opposite end of the see-saw, it can be a massive problem.

My family felt as if we had a joy deficit. There was a lack of laughter and play. I took it upon myself to be the bringer of joy and the one who could lighten the load of others. In translation, this meant ironing, making early morning tea for my mum, carrying the shopping bags, unloading the shopping, unpacking the shopping and generally picking up all small tasks that an 8-year-old could handle. I was hypervigilant—ready to pounce when I saw the energy drop.

Since being unwell, I have spent days and weeks delving inside. I've sat with one core question: Who am I apart from my history and the roles I have played? Like many people, the first half of my life was spent constructing and maintaining my persona. I sought out knowledge, more knowledge, influence and success. Up up up! It is only now, following my crisis and cataclysmic descent that I am seizing the permission to live my full potential. It means me going back and picking up what was left behind; the *joie de vivre*, the hopes, the untapped talent. The play that I never got to have. Yes, my freedom to play.

I will never know, but had I not become ill, would I have continued to garner more knowledge because that is what one does?! This outdated belief keeps many of us wedded to the quest for ascent.

Deep play is seductive for me. It is starting to appear in a few ways, mostly creative: photography, songwriting, poetry. And pottery. Yep, ceramics. Both admiring the work of others and getting stuck into clay and crafting my own. When I sit at the wheel, I'm alive. Nothing else matters in that moment more than the relationship I have with the clay and the opportunity to be the midwife to something of beauty.

make memories and
wonder and wander this plane
through your fleeting life

This is my life. I have just this one. I get the opportunity to run wild across the planet in some funny looking skin suit, in my case named Richard, and then I'll die. And then, depending on your narrative, like Mr Benn in the fancy dress shop, I get to choose my next skin suit (human, animal, plant …) But, for now, here I am. Richard Tyler. My life.

But how have I used it? Has it been to the benefit and service of others? Have I been kind? Have I grabbed opportunities? Have I *made* opportunities? Have I fully lived this one rich and precious life?

Amongst appointments for bloodletting, injections, chemo cycles and bouts of both vomit and diarrhoea, I have asked these questions on numerous occasions. Cancer is a leveller. At least it has been for me. It grabbed me by the shoulders and turned me around, facing into my life path and my soul. It held me there whilst I looked. When I squeezed my eyes shut, it prised them back open with hot tweezers. There was no averting my gaze from this life. The lived. The present. The future.

Like most people, I have lists. Lists of lists. Lists of things to see. Places to venture. Feelings to feel. Streams of experiences that I want to welcome into my heart for safe keeping. And for me, like many people, they remain untouched. They will probably stand, like stone statues, enduring the test of time. They will live under the guise of *shoulds*. Perhaps, one day, they will be elevated to *could haves*. Or, placed in the *if only I'd* catalogue.

Cancer is not going to turn me into someone who leaps out of bed at 6 am and crams the day with activity. I don't suddenly have any urges to climb big hills. But I will savour what I come across. I will breathe it in and let it find a place within me. And yes, I'll go out and seek more beauty. More awe. More wonder. It exists in both the magnificent and the mundane.

I am beginning to let more *reach me*. What reached you today?

AUTUMN

mono no aware: a Japanese idiom that reminds us that everything in existence is temporary—the changing of seasons are not to be mourned, but cherished and appreciated in their impermanence, for that is where their beauty comes from

The time of year that Keats called the 'Season of mists and mellow fruitfulness'. Autumn is a season famous for its harvest time, turning leaves, cooling temperatures and darkening nights. With the first signs of festive goodies filling our supermarket aisles, it is apparent that autumn is here to greet us; our woodland puts on a thrilling display of gold and crimson leaves, dazzling us with their beauty; the fiery hues of autumn are unmissable; the nightingales, cuckoos and swallows head south in search of warmer climes; redwings, waxwings and some ducks make their way towards the UK in hope of finding cooler air; sweet juicy blackberries cry out to us to pluck them from the bushes; soon the hedgerows will be groaning with other mouth-watering delights too—keep a lookout for ripe elderberries, sloes and wild raspberries; ivy is one of the few plants left to flower at this time; plump acorns and shiny brown conkers nestle in the leaf litter at your feet; dead man's fingers and lemon disco are just two of the fabulous fungi that could capture your imagination. Our natural world puts on such a spectacle for us.

Autumn always feels like a liminal space; the long walk between gentle summer days and chilly winter nights. A time that falls firmly *in between*. Our T-shirts can't quite be packed away but we're not ready for duffle coats and long johns just yet either. This season entices us into a period of change and we begin to shed the old, in order that we can make way for the new. A time to focus on the impermanence of life, acknowledging how vital it is to embrace the present. Autumn is a time to hunker down, retreat indoors and focus on cultivating a safe and comforting home ahead of the winter. Immunity boosting is vital to ensure good health during the colder months.

The autumn equinox gives us days and nights of equal length. Use this time as one of restoring balance that may have been lost.

My own lost balance returns in glimmers. Some days serve to remind me that winter is never far away. As I begin to build strength, time spent in nature supports my body's capacity for healing.

in my letting go
i fall into the abyss
and will be reborn

Having a stem cell transplant (SCT) was, for me, an alarming prospect. I could die. Quite literally, I could be carried out in a box. Call me dramatic, and yet it happens. Have you ever watched the documentary *Man on Wire*? It's horrifying. Walking a high wire, more than 1,300 ft up in the air. I mean, why …?! When I first saw it, I imagined that in order for him to be with his fear, he had to let go. Release any and all attachments and expectations. For Philippe Petit, the man at the heart of *Man on Wire*, a fall from that height meant instant death. A fall for me during my SCT would leave me brushing up close to death too. It could all go very wrong and yet, I knew I must let go. I had to loosen the tight hold I wanted to have on my life. Jeez, who am I kidding, the tight hold I *had* on my life.

Soon after my SCT, I received messages from a young lady called Gemma. She was in hospital herself, isolated during her transplant. She wanted to know how she could best manage the pain and bleakness of it all. We chatted. She was in her thirties with a partner and two young boys at home. For about a week, she fell silent. I checked in but no reply. A week later her partner messaged me to say she had picked up an infection and passed away. He wanted to relay how grateful she was for our message exchange. How crushing. An entire family life brought to its knees. My own system went into shock. Who caught Gemma when she fell?

My deepest fear was that should I fall, there was no bottom to the pit. So, who would catch me? Would anyone be there in my moment of greatest need? Maybe these form some of the questions that one asks when they are faced with their own mortality. When the answers come it is too late to bring any comfort. So, only if I moved beyond the fears within this belief could I let go …

Who catches you? If you fell, who would stand fiercely alongside you, no matter what? Find your kin. Find your catchers. At some moment in time, when faced with descent, you will need them.

acting like a plague
you unsettle everything
assassinating the love

I believe I have a strong sense for sniffing out a 'smiling assassin' amongst the crowd. You maybe know the type. They bathe you in charm but there is a serrated edge to their intentions. An edge that will take you down if you dare to blink. Unpredictable. Inconsistent. Overflowing entitlement. Empathy in short supply. Exquisite liars.

I am fortunate that I have many people in my life who offer an expanse of love and kindness. I have a few smiling assassins too. In fairness, most of them I have managed to lose along the way. But not all. One remains. Harder to shake off. Their rusty blade still has the power to cut deep within my own heart and the hearts of those I love most.

I cannot control them. And I cannot delete them. So, I focus on protection and damage limitation. I am learning to shield myself so that whilst they may wield their blade, I don't let it make contact. At this moment in my adventure, energy is at a premium. It is a rich currency that I find I can quickly burn through so I've done a deal with myself; sift with care and stand firmly in the centre of my human right to say no. NO! I grew up saying yes and feeling an obligation to please, regardless of how it affected me.

I wonder if the porous nature of us humans means that we often absorb more than is good for us. Sharpening our instrument of awareness must surely be a good thing for us all.

Love is precious and demands that we treat it accordingly. It is worth knowing who the assassins are in your life. And it is from here that you are better placed to stand firmly in the power of your YES, and your NO.

as the church bells toll
mourners bear the mighty grief
hair how i miss thee

My hair had become more popular and iconic than I was. Yes, it was an extension of me, sure. But in some ways, my quiff had forged its own career and lifestyle. It was only missing its own Instagram account.

I am ashamed to admit it, but my hair was the cause of great stress and turmoil in my life. I would spend hours pruning and preening before an event. On reflection, it was painful. How did I ever become so obsessed with my image? Regardless, I was. Oh, and then I got cancer. And suddenly, it wasn't quite so important.

When I knew I was about to start treatment and certain that my hair loss was looming, I needed to seize control. This meant getting it shaved off before my lymphoma stole it. I'm grateful that Mia was fairly breezy about the whole 'can you shave my head' scenario. It helped me make this entire shitshow a little less shitty.

To you, this might all sound a bit over the top. I look back and wonder how my obsession with my hair ever took hold. Letting go of obsession is freeing. Detaching from the idea that I am who I am due to my hair allowed me to place down the very heavy load I had carried. I hold some grief for it, yes. I was Samson. Seeing my bald head smiling back at me each day was symbolic of the loss of strength I felt and the rich comfort that is found in familiarity.

Quiff. RIP.

**anchovy and jam
a Blumenthal recipe
the taste of cancer**

I'm wondering what parts of my body cancer didn't wreak havoc with. No sooner was I into my chemo regime, the funny tastes began. My most favourite tea was suddenly rank. Peanut butter and marmite—vomit! To be fair, for many people, PB and marmite might bring about instant vomiting, without the aid of chemo! For me, it's top of my go-to list. I even once thought about setting up a club for PB&M lovers. But eventually thought better of it as I reckoned it would be a pretty lonely place with just one member.

Days after cycle 1 of drugs, my imagination kicked in. And I was off. All kinds of fabulously odd tastes and cravings swilled around my mouth. It was a hammam for my taste buds! I longed for dishes that my mother had made when I was growing up; Shepherd's pie with baked beans, Cod in parsley sauce, Liver and Bacon.

My poor Kelly. She would be at the shops every day in a desperate attempt to find something I might enjoy eating and drinking. We considered setting up a corner shop to sell the unwanted, half-eaten goods. But we don't live on a corner, so we packed that idea in.

As the days have passed and my taste has some semblance of order again, I appreciate the flavour bombs that go off in my mouth. What a privilege it is to bask in the taste of food and drink. Whilst it remains more subdued than I recall, it is thankfully on its way back.

Cancer was guiding me to voyage far into my body. I had, for so long, mostly occupied my head. At each turn, it was as if my soul was trying to steer me back to my essence. And what could be closer to pure essence than being fully immersed in your body? I swerved the anchovies and jam but, at some point, I may well consider it for my next club idea.

i might push you back
i will push you back
see i pushed you back

One of the toughest parts of my psychotherapy training was learning to set firm boundaries; with self and with clients. I've always had a flaky relationship with boundaries. We never really got on. Life had taught me that YES was better than NO. Saying no led to disappointment, upset and guilt. My dad set boundaries at work, but not at home. My mum melted when a boundary of hers was compromised—she felt sadness and distress when someone told her No! Often, her only way forwards was to guilt and shame the other, in some vague hope that No, would eventually morph into Yes.

If cancer had rocked up to my home to teach me anything, it was to help me see the power of my Yes *and* my No. And what better time to start learning about boundaries than when you need them most.

I stepped tentatively. Often with trepidation. The fear of the other person's upset at facing into my NO would render me frozen. But I started small. I will always be a work in progress as I find the best ways to swim through the choppy rip tide that can suck you from the surface deep into the undercurrents. It requires greater consciousness. When I switch on autopilot, a resounding no is unlikely.

There is little more liberating than using your free pass which entitles you to swerve the sense of obligation, and stand resolute in your No. I have found it life-changing. In fact, it is life-giving.

Which do you stand in more often, your YES, or your NO? By the way, one isn't better than the other. Far from it. Both are essential if we wish to travel well.

past my line of sight
you are called to travel on
i'm forced to let go

Sometimes I wonder if Kelly and I were utterly bonkers to have started a blood cancer charity at the same time as venturing through our own sticky cancer adventure. It's one thing facing your own mortality and understanding how brittle and delicate life can be, but starting a charity that will bring you closer to the death of others is perhaps wildly foolish.

Soon after my own diagnosis, I mean a matter of days, a friend of mine sent me a message to tell me she had been diagnosed with triple negative breast cancer. She didn't want me to tell anyone as only a few people knew and she was not yet feeling brave enough to share her news. Jo and I were walking a similar path. Similar and different. After all, no two cancer journeys are the same. Kelly and I supported Jo to find integrative approaches that might just enable her to make a few small steps towards good health again. She was my age. Had a zest for life and a daughter the same age as Mia—they had been at primary school together. Jo had every good reason to live.

Eight months later, as Kelly and I gathered with her family and friends to celebrate her life and lay her to rest, I couldn't help but wonder if I should have gone with her. I mean, we'd set out on this path together, so what happened? I stopped and watched her walk on. Our shared grip on life was loosened. Her hand slipped from mine and she was called forward.

Jo was determined to live. She was adamant that she would see her daughter turn 18. She didn't. Jo, wherever you now wander,

I hope you do so free of the pain and loss that you were tormented with in your final months.

I sense the act of holding someone close and then acknowledging the time to let them go is one of the most gruelling tasks of being human. And one of the most necessary.

his shit-filled nappy
the wonder of being born
but i'm forty nine

S tem cell transplants (SCT) are a fairly commonplace intervention with lymphoma. They work like this (possibly the most non-medical description you might ever read—do not try this at home!). A super-duper Doctor Who gadget removes my blood from one arm, spins it in a centrifugal machine thingy, takes the cells it needs and returns the rest into my other arm. It's called harvesting, except they don't use a combine harvester. It takes around 5 hours; 2 weeks later, I go into hospital (for 4 weeks of total isolation in the same room with no visitors). First, they obliterate my body with chemotherapy drugs. It strips me of everything my body has left. Next, they take my harvested cells and pop them back into my body. Boom. Job done. A breeze. Not.

It's savage. The 4 weeks were by far the toughest of my life. A challenge I didn't ask for. Well, not consciously anyway. Doctors refer to SCTs as being reborn. Your body is wiped like a hard drive. Every childhood inoculation, gone. SCT-ers refer to their *re-birthday* on the day the cells are given back.

So, here I was. 49 years old. A fairly well-functioning adult human being with a wife, a daughter, a mortgage and a business. And I'm lying in bed like a newborn baby, unable to control when its own shit is ejected from its back passage. Yep, that was me. Given an adult nappy to wear because I had filled the entire bed with my faeces. It was like I could no longer be trusted. If I couldn't control when I crapped, it was surely the end of my independence.

Here was my crucible. A drastic test of my resolve. I was forced back to the starting line. Yet I was so far through my race. Being called back to the beginning, expected to start over, is gut-wrenching. In that moment, the last thing we want to do is to relive what has already been lived. But what is impossible to see at the time is that we get to do this thing called life again. But this time, with wisdom. We are already so practised, we can go forwards to live from a place of far greater choice.

I was handed the bag of my own cells. I was given a pen and a notebook and the opportunity to write a new story. My new story. Perhaps, a better one.

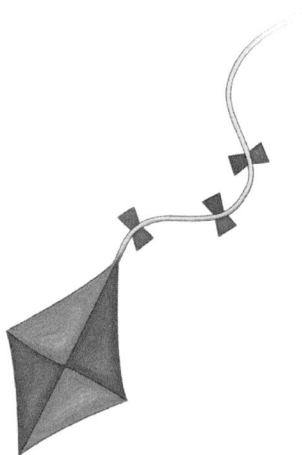

Travel consciously

For about 5 years of my life, I was fortunate enough to travel to every continent of this planet, delivering workshops to leaders and organisations on The Art of Possibility with my company BTFI. Along with professional musicians Al Gurr and Sara Colman, we would pack keyboards, speakers and a whole raft of kit, before boarding planes to jet off. Our aim was to touch lives and provoke organisations to play differently. Every trip was crammed full of experiences ranging from utterly terrifying right through to astoundingly beautiful. We would eventually arrive back at the airport, full to the brim with memories and ready to head to our homes and back to family. We'd place down our luggage, give big hugs, share our thanks and appreciation and go our separate ways. Our lives forever changed.

I feel like our adventure, yours and mine, is not dissimilar. Together, we have shared this path. These past pages have revealed intimate moments that only the two of us will have lived through. Writing this story has soothed my heart. It has afforded me the space and time to begin making sense of how I include the ascent and descent of my own life. My hope is that by walking this path with me, you have also been moved in some way that will leave your life in a slightly better way than when we first met. And now is the time where we both place down the stories, the questions and the revelations from this shared adventure, we hug it out and we say our goodbyes.

Thank you for travelling with me. I am grateful that you trusted in something enough to pick this book up and give it a go. Maybe some of the love and the moments contained within will find a way into the stories that you take forward and share with others. Feel free to pass them on. Perhaps you will even start writing your own haiku! Whatever you choose to do next, thank you. Walk with hope and love. Go well.

With love and gratitude

Richard x

Epilogue

I was fortunate to be with my dad when he passed away in December 2011. I watched him draw his final breath. His last expulsion of air. My dad's parting sigh to the world. His body and soul were wracked with exhaustion from 9 months of illness, but now it was all over. The fat lady had sung her final note. The curtain fell. His last step through *descent.* As I looked at his face, I could see a smile trickle across, almost as if he'd acknowledged the joy that he'd discovered, amongst his pain. Perhaps, after all, he had himself learnt that *ups* and *downs* do, indeed, sit side by side. And so for one last time, his kite soared. Love you Dad.

Acknowledgements

When, in the wee small hours, a party ends and the majority of guests head off, there are always a few who hang around to help clear up the party aftermath. These are the committed souls who stay to the bitter end to scrape quiche off the carpet and pick soufflé off of the sofa. When the glitz and sparkle have finished, they remain staunchly by your side. Well, this section is to thank as many of you as I can who have stayed in my life, way after the ending of the party.

The birthing of a book is not easy. A writer pours their heart and soul into the work. Finding enough fortitude and will to bring it to life is, therefore, a mighty task. If it weren't for some very meticulous and generous bundles of talent, this book would have remained an unfertilised egg.

Kate and the Karnac team—thank you for believing in me and this book. I couldn't have wished for a more caring, attentive and gifted team to help me birth my baby!

Rebecca—I am blessed to have you in my corner, cheering me on. I cannot tell you how much your insight and all-round writing genius has helped me.

Laura—I am deeply grateful for you and the way in which you have brought my childhood to life through your beautiful art.

Brett—over 35 years ago, you saw a talent in me and had the faith that I was a good choice for your singing group. That faith has held the test of time. I am eternally grateful to you for the wisdom and support you show me.

Susan (my therapist), you have remained alongside me at every step of this adventure. Your huge heart and abundance of kindness that you have showered on me is priceless.

Charlie—thank you for reminding me that there are young trailblazers on our planet who not only stand in their own truth, but do so with love and kindness.

Carolina—the blurred lines between corporate client and deep friendship matter not. Your enormous optimism, zest for life and capacity to love has helped me find my way through some very tricky days.

Rita (my GCSE English teacher), thank you for helping me scrape through my GCSE English exam, despite some extremely ropey pieces of writing.

Tony and Lin (my GCSE drama teachers), thanks for taking a punt on some kid who said they wanted to be an actor. You encouraged me at the very time when I could so easily have walked away. Your boundless zest for life and enthusiasm for storytelling lives on in me. Thank you for believing in my ability to bring stories to life.

John O'Donohue and David Whyte for revealing the beauty in words.

Roberto Assagioli, thank you for your discoveries and your belief in the importance of synthesis. As each day passes, I look to synthesise all aspects of my life.

Dearest Edwin—your unwavering support, energy and spiritual guidance continues to hold me firm. I remain in gratitude.

For my family who have shown such commitment and compassion to us all here in Tyler Towers. These past months have tested you too and, for your unwavering love, there are few words that can express my gratitude.

Mum—I doubt you will read this. I'm still waiting for you to read my last book! You have been my cheerleader and champion for over 50 years. Thank you.

David—you are ever present, and that means everything.

Sue—I am grateful for the way you always drop things to support us on this topsy-turvy adventure. I value your artistic talent and the way you brought each seasonal page to life with your wonderful drawings.

Steve and Kaz—there is never a day where we don't feel your love and support.

Royston, you cannot imagine the constant source of joy that you are for me.

My Mia, you are the light in my life. I live to see the tremendous impact you will have on this world. I will be cheering you on with deep pride, always.

My Kelly, there are few words to express how much you mean to me. My life is far better with you in it. Thank you for remaining by my side, at the darkest of times. I love you.

To each doctor, hospital cleaner, nurse, healthcare assistant, consultant, physio, radiographer, acupuncturist, oncologist, member of The Princess Alice Hospice and the people who cooked my food in hospital, I am still here because of you.

And finally, to everyone who has walked, is currently walking and at some point will walk this path alongside cancer, it's a toughie. I won't lie. Find your tribe who will hold you up. I, for one, will be a part of that tribe.